Some Commentary
on the
Philosophy and Practice
of
Phineas Parkhurst Quimby

by

ERVIN SEALE

TIDE PRESS
P.O. BOX 4224
LINDEN, NEW JERSEY 07036

MINGLING MINDS.

FIRST EDITION   First Printing

ISBN 0-912931-04-3

Contents

Phineas Parkhurst Quimby

Ervin Seale

Preface

A valued friend and advisor once remarked, "I can't read Quimby but I can read Seale. Why doesn't Seale write about the main ideas of Quimby." So Seale did and this book is the result.

As the work developed it took on two purposes. First, to serve as a guide to the study of the Quimby writings, so that if the new reader or the old-and-still-puzzled-reader encounters familiar words with unfamiliar meanings, he can turn to this commentary and read what another has made of them.

Quimby himself wrote several introductions to a prospective book he planned to publish, for he realized that some people would find difficulty in seeing "some meaning in his otherwise blind writings. . . .if no explanation or introduction to his writings is made, the reader would of course pass over what he says with indifference and condemn it as visionary."

In order to avoid a dreary repetition of Quimby's words, the author has introduced material of his own and others to illustrate and clarify the concepts of Quimby and has rephrased those concepts in more modern words by which the reader may grasp Quimby's thought more quickly. Unless otherwise noted, all quotations of Quimby are double indented and in italics. Words in brackets are mine.

The book's second purpose, as it turned out, is to serve as a spiritual manual, a handbook of a way of thinking to enrich the personal life of the reader.

New York, N.Y.   *Ervin Seale*
April, 1986

Is It All In Your Mind?

It is not among the kindest of remarks to say to the ailing person, "It's all in your mind." Certainly it is not the truest. For what is most often implied by such a statement is that the pain is not real, that the sufferer imagines it. This is nonsense and the sufferer knows it. If you feel a pain, you know that you do, whatever its source and cause. To say that pain is "just imagination" is to belittle and sully the word and faculty of imagination by suggesting that imagination is an airy, dreamy and unreal fancy. Whereas, in all truth, the imagination is the creative faculty of mind. Ideas are the beginnings of all things and imagination is the faculty that engineers them into form and function. Unfortunately, among humankind, the imagination is much more skillful in digging holes than in rearing structures of peace and happiness.

> *I tell you a lie and you believe it, immediately your inventive power or imagination commences to create that which I have said. I explain the oper-ation of a machine to you and your inventive power immediately creates it according as you understand it. This is imagination.   I never use the word*

as others do. When people think they have a disease which I know they do not, I do not ascribe it to their imagination, but to the fact that they have been deceived.

Phineas Parkhurst ("Park" to his neighbors) Quimby's method of treating the sick was to sit by them and render himself absent to everything but the patient's feelings.   This clockmaker and inventor from Belfast, Maine, speaking of himself in the third person, says, "*These* [the patient's feelings] *are daguerreotyped* [he was an early daguerreotypist. . . .one of the first successful cameras was invented by Da Guerre] *on him. They contain no intelligence, but shadow forth a reflection of themselves which he looks at. This contains the disease as it appears to the patient. Being confident that it is the shadow of a false idea, he is not afraid of it, but laughs at it. Then his feelings in regard to the disease, which are health and strength, are daguerreotyped on the receptive plate of the patient, which also throws forth a shadow and he sees the change and continues to treat it in the same way. So the patient's feelings sympathize with his, the shadow grows dim and finally the light takes its place and there is nothing left of the disease.*"   Because of what he knew, Quimby was able to use his imagination constructively and he labored constantly to teach others how to do so. This is the way he "read" the patient's mental and psychic state and this is why I have called him the modern world's first true psychoanalyst for he did not ask the patient questions nor encourage him to babble about his complaints. Rather, he told the patient how he felt and why. Moreover, he was not guessing or "divining" but telling exactly what he saw with his spiritual eyes.

> *When I tell them how they feel, I tell them it is in their mind. This of course they do not believe. . . . a great many people think that I believe all disease is of the imagination but this is wrong. I always admit disease for it is what I feel and that is real.*

The distinction between Quimby's concept and the common view of disease is in the definition. What is commonly called disease is a symptom or symptoms in the flesh, a pain or dysfunction in the body. Quimby called that the effect of a deception in the mind.

> *This deception I call the disease and*

> *the effect that follows they* [doctors]*call
> the disease.*

He relates that it was common in his day, as it certainly is in ours, to hear someone say, "It's all in your mind" or another to say, "I wasn't thinking about a cold so it could not be in my mind." Quimby throws light on this confusion by showing that sickness is in the mind, not in the sense that you are thinking sickness, but rather in the sense that what you are thinking may be making you nervous, anxious or fearful or angry or sad. These states of mind are *dis*-ease. They produce disease.   Two persons may think the same thought. One is frightened; one is not. The former is closer to disease.

> *Idiocy is not disease for a fool is
> perfectly satisfied.*

The concept that pain is "all in your mind" and therefore unreal did not come from Quimby but rather from some of his followers who did not quite understand his theory. Their views are what one of Quimby's friends, a patient and early biographer, Mrs. Julius (Annetta) Dresser, mother of Horatio and author of *The Philosophy of P. P. Quimby*, called "the derived teachings." The idea of "mind over matter" is a derived teaching for Quimby did not divide mind from matter but called mind spiritual matter.

Thus what people usually call disease—the pain or distress or malfunction in the body—is not the disease but rather the effect of the disease. The disease is the disturbed mind.   This distinction is fundamental and gives strength to the mind in handling any problems.

> *What we see* [body, form, function, action, etc.] *has as much to do with the man as the engine of a steamboat lying at a wharf in Portland with the intelligence of the maker in New York.*

In other words, the engine did not make itself. Some intelligence made it and that intelligence can make other engines like it. So with the body or the affairs of a person. What you see is the result of something you don't see. What you don't see is a kind of thinking. The intelligence of the maker, of steamboat or human body, is of first importance. Suppose a certain mind accepts and believes the common view that disease is independent of the person, that it acts of itself.

*Did you ever see the liver complaint
walking around by itself?*

This is what Quimby would call a belief or an opinion as opposed to a truth, and because beliefs manifest or express themselves automatically and without our conscious knowledge, we do not detect the cause within ourselves and suppose it to be outside. In his early experiments with his subject, Lucius Burkmar, "*I found that not only my thoughts but also my beliefs affected my subject. If I really believed a thing, the effect would follow whether I was thinking of it or not.*"

This question confronts each person then. What do you believe? And how do you know what you believe? Since believing is largely subconscious, the question cannot be adequately answered by citing the Christian Creed or some other statement of religious belief for one may not really believe in his heart what he says with his mouth. Do you believe that disease is independent, that the liver complaint can walk around by itself, that cancer exists by itself and can have an effect on you without your allowance? If you do, then this belief can act subconsciously and establish conditions and situations which you do not want. And if you do believe this then you do not "believe on him."

All of this brings us back to the ancient land-mark: "the fruits of the spirit [right thinking] are love, joy, peace, longsuffering, gentleness, good-ness, faith, meekness and temperance." Against such there is no law—no restraint, prohibition or punishment. Is the mind at peace with its concepts? Then there is no disease and there can be no disturbed condition in the body. Think thoughts that cause these emotions to flourish and you can't be sick. But human existence requires the meeting and reconciliation of oppo-sites. So every mind has to deal at times with error, illusion, deception and turmoil. In the myths the hero has to walk *through* the fire unharmed to retrieve the lost or the holy or to awaken the sleeping maiden or the true self.

A modern physician, Arnold Fox, M.D., and author of the famous Beverly Hills Diet says that his years of research and practice have shown him that the people who have lived very long and happy lives have six crucial personality traits: enthusiasm, moderation, serenity, optimism, interest in the future and interest in others. On the other hand, depression, pessimism, and dis-paraging thoughts and attitudes work against you and your health. Dr. Fox answers that knotty question of how thought becomes flesh by showing how your brain turns your thought and attitudes into chemical messengers (hormones) which circulate through your body. In effect your body becomes a mirror of your mind. When one is depressed, a certain set of depression chemicals race through the body. The body responds to these depressing chemicals by becoming fatigued and sleepy, restless, apathetic, sore and so on. When one is happy, enthusiastic and optimistic, the brain circulates "up" chemicals through the body. These "up" chemicals give you a mental and physical lift. You feel alive, vibrant and strong.

The persons with the six crucial personality traits are more likely to live "young and healthy to a very old age." While the depressed person's thought actually turn into chemicals which depress the immune system, the enthusiastic person's thoughts actually strengthen his resistance to disease. We shall have more to say about this modern research if and when we deal with Quimby's concept of changing the fluids of the system by thought.

One of the most destructive acts of the human

mind that I have seen in my experience is scorn. I have seen promising business relationships destroyed, marriages ruined and bodies debilitated by this self-demeaning act of the mind. I say self-demeaning because this emotion, unbeknownst to the one who indulges it, reduces himself or herself while he or she thinks he is cutting down another. Its cousins are envy and disdain and belittlement and hate and self-pride and rancor of all kinds. Surely that is why the psalmist dealt with this first in his one hundred and fifty songs of hope and praise: "Blessed is the man who walketh not in the counsel of the ungodly, nor standeth in the way of sinners, nor sitteth in the seat of the scornful."

One could trace the devastating effect of scorn in the lives of individuals and nations, for it has wasted many throughout history. Those who are delivered from it have their interest and delight in what the psalmist calls the law of the Lord (or the executive power of mind and thought) and this is where P. P. Quimby's interest and delight were. Over and over he emphasizes that disease is not independent but a state of the mind. It is a part of a person's knowing.

Where is the cancer if there is no person?

From 1843 to 1847 Quimby was a practicing mesmerist. He traveled with Lucius Burkmar through the small towns of Maine and New Brunswick lecturing and giving exhibitions on mesmerism. Lucius kept a daily journal and on one day he writes, "Quimby has been doing miracles. He has cured a man that couldn't walk nor speak." In the next chapter we shall discuss Quimby's first experiment with Lucius. Lucius became the foil or mirror through which Quimby could observe the workings of mind—his own and that of others. He saw his ideas take form and concluded that man had the power of creation. Therefore man is himself the cause of his experience. There is no god to punish him. His reward and his punishment are in himself. Scorn and rancor are not possible to the mind that knows this. On the contrary, delight and enthusiasm are its constant content. The person whose delight is in this law of things knows that envy and scorn and all their pernicious cousins are forms of psychological self-denial—not in the same way as when Jesus says, "Deny yourself," etc., but in the sense that his emotion minimizes the self, denies its worth and invites hurt and sorrow while blaming a fictitious "other."

Is it all in your mind? Most certainly, because it

cannot be anywhere else. Where there is no mind, there can be no experience. Did the tree fall last night when there was no one there to see it? To the universal mind, Yes. To the individual mind, No, for the individual mind's experience is local. Once in awhile, however, the individual mind escapes its individual confines and then its experience is enhanced and widened. We shall expand this idea later in this volume .

For now we shall continue to emphasize and enlarge and deepen the understanding that pain is in the mind in a particular sort of way. Not in the way of the usual, popular conception, but in the peculiar and precise sense that Quimby explains. Troward has said, "If a thing is true, there is a way in which it is true." Let us be sure to see the way in which Quimby's statement is true.

The Quimby writings frequently recall the case of the young army captain who had been wounded in the wrist by a minnie ball and whose arm had been amputated below the elbow. He still felt the pain of the wound and it caused him much suffering. Although the surgeons had removed the arm, they had not been able to remove the pain. Today, doctors call this a phantom pain.

Now where was the pain? It was not in the arm for the arm was gone. It was not in the flesh or matter for there was none. He felt pain in his arm but he had no arm. Where was the pain? It was in his mind and it was real. He felt it and suffered from it. It was not in his mind in the sense of imagination or delusion, but rather in his mind as a strong impression persisting from the day when he had a healthy arm and the arm was shot. The mind is a medium for two kinds of intelligence or information. Quimby often calls them two directions. Intelligence comes from two sources: the environment or material world and the immaterial world or from the world of form and the world of formlessness or spirit. The biblical words for these two are heaven and earth. Repeated impressions from the same source become established as assumptions and presumptions and with repeated emphasis become obsessions and fixed states of mind. Today we refer to these fixed states of mind as being subconscious, but the term was not current in Quimby's time. His way was to distinguish between thoughts as the conscious function of mind and beliefs as the subconscious function.

> *I found that my own thoughts were one thing and my belief another. If I really*

believed in anything, the effect would follow whether I was thinking of it or not.

When a child is born, its eager and loving parents watch with fascination as the child orients its senses outward and gathers impressions of the external world. It responds to sights and sounds and "feels" and gradually "grows up." Some say the child is learning. Others say it is acquiring bonds. At any rate, it soon gets attached to certain ideas and these become fixed, often for life. It has been observed that "many young people have stopped learning in the. . . .spiritual dimensions of their lives long before they graduate from college. Some settle into rigid and unchanging political and economic views by the time they are twenty-five or thirty. By their mid-thirties most will have stopped acquiring new skills or new attitudes in any central aspect of their lives." (John W. Gardner, *Self-Renewal*). Quimby described this process of fixation as "*attaching one's senses to an idea.*"

To go back to the army captain with the severed arm, we can see that his senses were attached to the idea of an arm. His senses had not yet attached themselves to the idea of a lost arm. The physical arm had been removed but his senses still retained the awareness or sensation of an arm, and that is why he felt pain. Quimby took hold of the stump and carefully explained the situation.

> *The stump he did not feel, but the hand was as real as the other. . . . he felt the hand and the doctor could not change his mind by telling him that the hand was gone. This was false in the true sense, for his hand was a part of his senses and the phenomenon that could be seen was nothing to his senses; he had a hand and it troubled him. . . .So I took hold of the stump and by explaining the truth, I changed the mind and he cast the idea away and then felt of the stump and became quiet, satisfied that it was better to have one arm and be happy and well than having two and be in torment.*

Now if Quimby had been as unable as the doctors to change the captain's mind, he could not have got rid of the pain and misery. His pain was in his mind.

In this chapter we have tried to establish and embellish one of the main concepts of P. P. Quimby's philosophy and science and practice, namely, that disease is not independent of the mind, cannot and does not exist by itself, and that sickness follows the belief that disease is an independent life.   Where, he asks, was the disease before you knew about it?   Mind the knower is also mind the maker.

> *So when I say the disease is in the mind, I mean that it does not exist anywhere else.*

This understanding lights up the mind in freedom, banishes a thousand devilish fears and restores the mind to its kingly confidence.

2

What Is Mind?

What is mind? An ancient Chinese answer could be: "Nobody knows." Mental functions give evidence of the mind but the mind itself is beyond description. It is like a light in the darkness. It make visible a variety of objects and scenes but it, itself, is unknown. Perhaps that is why so much is written about it, but there is no precise definition of mind in our literature. Consult a dictionary or thesaurus and you may be told that mind is intellect and intellect means intelligence and intelligence means having knowledge and having knowledge is knowing and knowing is consciousness and consciousness is mind and presently you come out the same door wherein you went. Philosophers throughout history have confused mind, soul and spirit.

That is the way it is now and that is the way it was in the early nineteenth century when Quimby began to investigate the ways of the mind and to find out what mind was.

> One of my first objects was to discover what mind is, for if the mind dies with the body, then all the fuss and trouble of living and using our minds would

*not be of importance hereafter and
would be of no value, so I made it my
first object of inquiry. . . . when I first
commenced operating on the mind I
put persons into a mesmeric state. . .
.at last I could make my subjects read
my thoughts and here was a new
discovery.*

On one occasion when he had put his subject, Lucius, to sleep he thought he would leave the room. Instantly the boy got up, went to the table and brought Quimby's hat.

*This was unexpected but it was just
what I wanted to know, if he could read
my thoughts. At first I was all aback,
but after recovering myself, I said to
myself, if you will replace my hat on
the table, I will stop a little longer.
Without saying a word, he sprang up,
took my hat and returned it to the table.
Here was another fact I had gotten, not
an opinion but a truth.*

What fact had he gotten? The fact that mind can talk to mind without words and language, what J. Allen Boone will call *The Language of*

Silence. Quimby will call it Thought-reading. It has been called Telepathy and Extra Sensory Perception. In that grouping of the Quimby writings called *The Lecture Notes* by Dr. Dresser in *The Quimby Manuscripts*, Quimby had already begun to develop a much broader concept of mind than any of his contemporaries or predecessors. Most of his contemporaries were explaining mesmeric phenomena as caused by a fluid or magnetism which was sent out by operator to subject. Quimby said it was the action of "mind on mind." Even at this stage, before the experiment with the hat, he was seeing mind as a receiver of impressions and a transmitter of the same. He will say that "our minds mingle," or "our atmospheres mingle." Thus you may be riding on a bus and suddenly feel fear or depression and not realize that it has nothing to do with you; you are picking it up from another. All things are "in the air" and are more or less perceived at any one time. Edison did not originate the electric light bulb nor Marconi the radio. They perfected them and brought the ideas into practical use. The ideas were "in the air" all over the world for years. Just as travel to the planets is "in the air" at this time and technology is creeping up apace.

This showed me that man has an

*unconscious power that is not
admitted [known or realized] which
governs his acts.*

Thus Quimby discovered what the French
hypnotists would later call the "double consciousness." There seemed to be two minds or two
levels of mind. All through the *Lecture Notes* he
refers to the mesmerized state as the "excited"
state and our ordinary waking mind he called the
standard state. Magnetizers were thought to
convey such a strong impression to a subject's
mind that the mind would be "thrown" or "excited"
into this state. Or suffering or worry could do it.
Psychologists gave these two states such names
as Conscious and Subconscious or Objective
and Subjective. Quimby has a dozen names for
them and a vastly more profound insight.

In these *Lecture   Notes*, after referring to a
number of philosophic and mesmeric writings of
the day and quoting their authors, sometimes at
length, Quimby takes up a number of peculiar
states of mind such as mesmerism, dreaming,
somnambulism, insanity and states of heightened
perception and shows that all these states of mind
are caused not by some external environmental
means but by the one means he sees governing

all mental phenomena: the action of "mind on mind."

One example of the kind of case that Quimby was reading about is the one of an officer who, while in this "excited" state, was a great source of amusement to his associates and friends. "*They could produce in him any kind of a dream by whispering in his ear. . . .at one time they conducted him through the whole progress of a quarrel which ended in a duel; and when the parties were supposed to be met, a pistol was placed in his hand, which he fired and was awakened by the report.*" On another occasion they found him asleep on the top of the locker or bunker in the cabin, where they made him believe he had fallen overboard and exhorted him to save himself by swimming.

These are fascinating accounts of what nowadays is called hypnosis. They are also fine examples of Quimby's proposition that mind is a medium for ideas and impressions and that "*man acts as he is acted upon.*" Quimby cites this case (above) from a book by a Dr. Abercrombie whose explanation he refutes:

> *The whispering in t he ear was only*

*whispering to the mind, the sense of
hearing, being, no doubt, inactive, and
all the expressions of the quarrel were
actually produced upon his mind and
not through the sense of hearing, by
the direction of those around him. . . .
all these impressions were the result
of mind acting upon mind—impressions conveyed by the minds of those
around him, directly to his mind, making precisely the same result, as
though he had in his waking state
fallen overboard. . . .*

Dr. Abercrombie relates an instance of a husband and wife dreaming the same dream at the same time. Recently they had witnessed in Edinburgh a splendid military spectacle. They had gone to bed excited and apprehensive over a threatened invasion. Between two and three a.m. the husband, who had been a zealous volunteer, dreamed he heard the signal gun. He was immediately at the castle. . . .and saw and heard a great bustle over the town from troops and artillery assembling in Princess Street. At this time he was aroused by his wife who awoke in a fright from having had a similar dream.

long about the time of Quimby's death (1866), hey demonstrated dramatically the existence of wo minds and the incredible power of suggestion. This was the term that would be current for the next fifty years to describe what Quimby called the "action of mind on mind." The researches of Professor Liebault and his pupil, Professor Bernheim, at the famous Nancy School, set the course. Their field of investigation was hypnotism, chiefly for therapeutic purposes. The Salpetrierre, presided over by Professor Charcot, also investigated hypnosis but took the position that it was a pathological state observable only in the sick.

Not far away in time but farther away in geography, the Russian, Pavlov, would show the conditioned reflex in dogs, and from him Soviet psychology would embark on its notorious and diabolical path of brainwashing to make people say and do against their will. For they reasoned that you could condition a person to do anything you willed. They did not realize how old this theory was and how often it had been used.

All, mesmerists, hypnotists and Quimby had made essentially the same discovery—the mind is constantly amenable to suggestion. In one way

Dr. Abercrombie attributed all this remarkable occurrence to a noise produced in the room above by the fall of a pair of tongs. *"But how,"* asks Dr. Quimby, *"should it happen that the tongs should have produced similar trains of thought in two different individuals?. . . .one would suppose that the noise would have been conveyed to the mind by the bodily senses, giving a true impression of its origin or at least would not have resulted in impressions so foreign to the real cause. The true explanation seems to be this. Both minds, no doubt, passed into the sleeping state, partially excited upon the alarm of the French invasion, etc. and were in the mesmeric sleep and in communication with each other, capable of giving and receiving impressions. The fall of the tongs might have affected the mind of one or both. It would not be necessary to affect more than one. The train of association is started in this highly excited state by an impression which could not have been given through the bodily senses. The impression received is immediately followed by other impressions connected with the subject upon which the mind was most intent during the waking state, and being in communication with the other, conveyed similar impressions but arising from* (as we would say in the waking state) *false causes."*

Here is Quimby, the clockmaker, who could calculate and fashion an intricate train of gears to keep the time; Quimby the inventor, who could think like an engineer, at home in mathematics and mechanics; and finally, Quimby, scientist of the mind, impatient with beliefs and opinions, perceiving the subtle ways of the mind as it works without the five senses. For the action of mind on mind is independent of those senses. No one before or since has matched his understanding. The learned ones of his day were hung up on the idea of a physical cause and so it is today. Ideas are like seeds. They lodge in the mind, germinate and grow up into "trees" and "cursed is everyone that hangeth on a tree." (Galatians 3:13 and Deuteronomy 21:23).

I maintain that all diseases are only known to exist as they affect the mind of the patient —that is, there would be no disease which could affect an individual provided it could not make a sensation on his mind. . . in cases of scrofula and what is sometimes termed King's evil, diseases said to be incurable, the power of the Seventh Son to cure them, is an effect upon the mind. . . . . . .

Slowly but surely it is borne in upon mind is not the brilliant intelligence that i thought to be. His discoveries showed mind is a medium for intelligence and inte is of two kinds: one positive and one ne He sees mind as a subtler form of matter be it is always changing. The mind that is writi is changing with the second hand. The min is reading this is also changing. The mind c present is not the mind of the previous h Every sight, sound, smell, touch and tast constantly bringing new intelligence about so thing. Every one of the five senses is caus changes in the receptive medium called the min This is why some psychologists have called th child mind a tabula rosa, a blank page on which ɑ thousand influences inscribe a hodgepodge of information—some good, some bad. Quimby saw it the same way but he did not use the scholarly phrase.

. . . .if he does not reason he is like a child, ready to be instructed by science OR opinions.

When the hypnotists followed the mesmerists

or another, this law has always been known since the time of the ancient witch doctor. The witch doctor built a fire in front of his hut and announced that when the smoke reached the door of a condemned person, he would die and he did—not from the smoke nor by the witch doctor's spell, but by his own acceptance of another's thoughts. Thousands of experiments have shown that a hypnotized person, by whatever means, cannot be made to do what he has not already accepted in his heart. All hypnosis is self-hypnosis.

> *What we believe, that we create. . . .If I really believed in anything, the effect would follow whether I was thinking of it or not.*

It is doubtful if there is any one more important piece of knowledge to be gained in human experience than this: the constant susceptibility of the mind to direction, true or false. As Thomson Jay Hudson put it in his benchmark study, *The Law of Psychic Phenomena*, "The subjective mind is constantly amenable to control by suggestion."

This law is dimly recognized in such phrases as "public opinion," "public relations," "propaganda," etc. In every week of the year, the Voice of America broadcasts 989 hours in forty-two languages, while in the same time the Moscow radio broadcasts 2175 hours in 81 languages. For what purpose? To get the ear and to condition the minds of millions of people. For in spite of dictators and totalitarian regimes, the collective will of the people rules. Kings could not and Presidents and Commissars cannot initiate or sustain a course of action without the support of public opinion. Therefore, it is necessary for politicians to influence the public mind. For the voice of the people is the voice of God (not in the sense that the people are always as right and as good as God, but rather in the sense that the collective will is the Making Power).

It is necessary and wise for the individual to work upon his own mind and give it a healthful direction. The Bible invites this: "Ask me of things to come and concerning the works of my hands command ye me." (Isaiah) Is it true that humans can command God? If so, in what way is it true? Certainly not in the way that men command other men, by dictation, judgment, statute, or by gossip and slander. In this law of the susceptibility of mind to direction, God, the Creator or the Making Power, has put himself before man as a servant:

"Concerning the works of my hands command ye me." Think of this some more. Think of it long and intently: God, the Almighty, has become man's servant and invites man to command him! Doesn't this seem incongruous? Impossible? Outlandish? It is all that until you realize the way in which it is true. God has made himself the servant of man by validating every human thought willy-nilly, good or bad. This shows man that God is with him (the Creator, Emanuel), that his rewards and his punishments are all from his own thought or belief. A little contemplation on this insight will show how the presence of so much evil in the world, far from being the puzzle it used to be is seen as a constructive force. In Quimby's words, it develops the Christ in man. Thus the genealogy of Christ is traced to the harlot and an old Midrashic source refers to it in this way: "Moab is come forth from lust; but Ruth shall come forth from Moab, and David from Ruth, and from David the Messiah."

Poor fearful humans, who see a demon in every shadow, a disease in every sneeze and destruction in every change, how can they know that they are themselves the cause of all that happens to them, until they note the effects of their own thought. All thought is creative for it gives direction to the mediumistic mind.   In our immaturity we believe that harm is outside us and that various forms of it, such as disease, for example, can attack us or affect us against our will.   And as we think, so it appears.   Until, hopefully, we lay aside that illusion for the insight that "as he thinketh in his heart, so is he."   Then the person no longer begs a God for favors nor cringes before a devil that doesn't exist.   The reason we are subject to both good and bad influences and the reason that both our negative and our affirmative thoughts are creative is that we may learn to measure the nature of our own thought and equate it with our experience.   "ye shall be as gods, knowing good and evil."   Man knows good and evil and is constantly troubled by what he knows.   Until he knows that this is the way of development and the more clearly he knows, the less pain is involved.   The pure gold is buried in the ore.   To get the gold, the ore must be crushed and smelted until the gold runs free. Quimby solved so many philosophic problems and this is one.   Why the evil in the world that God made?   To develop the Christ or the man that God made.

> *In my investigations I found that my*
> *ignorance   produced   phenomena*

which my wisdom could not correct.

Only the gods are free. The gods know good and evil and are untroubled. If Pharaoh and Egypt, which he ruled, represent the world, consider what dignity and power are conveyed to the individual in that divine announcement, "I have made thee a god to Pharaoh."

3

How Quimby Learned

*Quimby the Clockmaker Reborn
as the Mesmerist and the
Mesmerist Reborn as the Healer*

In November, 1843 when Quimby and Lucius were giving exhibitions of mesmerism in various towns, a letter was written by a citizen of Belfast, R. B. Allen, to Nathan Hale, Dr. Jacob Bigelow and Dr. John Ware of Boston. The letter concluded with these words: "Mesmerism as manifested by this boy lets in more light than any other window that has been opened for 1800 years."

Adding nearly 200 years, that statement is still remarkably and significantly true. In the following pages I shall try to indicate why I think so.

While Quimby's contemporaries were still alive, the hypnotists took over the field of his investigations. That is, the phenomena of artificial sleep began to be called hypnotism, so-called by James Braid, M.D., a Manchester surgeon. He called it hypnotism after the Greek god of sleep. He also showed that there was no "animal magnetism" or fluid involved, that suggestion, rather than passes and gestures, induced the sleep. Across the water in France, investigators like Binet, Fere, Janet and Charcot were studying the phenomena of "double consciousness" in hysterical individuals. Charcot founded the school of the Salpetrierre which held to the view that hypnosis is a form of artificial hysteria. They thought that only hysterical people could be hypnotized. By contrast, the founders of The Nancy School, Liebault and Bernheim, believed that the hypnotic condition was not analogous to hysteria, that it was a normal sleep or torpor. It has always seemed unfortunate to me that Freud when he studied hypnosis went to the Salpet-rierre rather than to Nancy. He concluded that hypnotism offered little in the way of learning how the mind works and went on to establish psycho-analysis. Since then western psychology largely ceased to give direction to the mind but instead has busied itself with exploring what was already deposited in the mind, especially in early child-hood. Pavlovian followers, on the other hand, have been vigorously pursuing the conditioning process, some of them believing that there is no limit to the control they can have over other men and nations but sadly missing one great dis-covery which Quimby made:

Every person has two identities: one

called the natural man and the other
the real man or God or Wisdom.

The natural man can be hypnotized, mesmerized, trained and conditioned in dozens of noble and diabolical ways but the real man is inviolable. A notable example of this was Cardinal Mindzenty. His captors and brainwashers did indeed break him. By forcing him to stand night and day under the blinding Klieg lights, without food and sleep, they forced him to say what they wanted him to say. But as soon as he was free of that devilish influence, the discipline his trained mind had long been taught to accept reasserted itself in power and majesty. There are other less notable examples of people who foiled the brainwashers' claim to absolute power over the human mind.

Gerald Heard once remarked that a laboratory rat is teachable and can be taught to eat the food that will kill it. A human, because he or she is teachable, can be taught a disastrous wrong. All animals can be trained to accept roles that man has chosen for them. Consider the circus where elephants dance and lions and tigers obey the whip and voice of a physically less powerful creature, man. In the teak forests of the East a mere eighty-pound man has trained a two-ton elephant to believe that it is inferior to the man. On command, it will lift the heavy log and place it where ordered. If once the truth should creep into the mind of that massive beast that the situation is ludicrous, that it is superior in strength and need not obey, then it would be free. But except for animals which go berserk, that never happens. The little man holds the big creature with the strongest chain there is, the effect of "mind on mind." Were it not for this principle of "mind on mind" or what the hypnotists called the "law of suggestion," no creature, man or beast, could ever be tamed or trained.

Also, this principle is the basis of nine tenths of human behavior. In city streets around the world there are marching groups shouting, "No more war!" Surely, a right and noble aspiration but one not to be achieved or fulfilled by simple decision. Humans do not go to war because they want to. They are compelled by unresolved conflicts within. Not until man achieves control over the war machine in himself will he be able to prevent nations from resorting to war. We boast of our free will but the least of us who has lost his temper will realize how little free will he has. Freedom of choice we have, but the power to maintain that choice is not always at hand.   Will power is the product of choice maintained. People don't do what they wish but what they must. All operate under a mind-set of some sort. "We are meat in which habits have taken up residence" (Salter). Paul saw this some centuries ago: "For the good that I would do I do not: but the evil which I would not, that I do." *Romans 7*

Consider the millions of honest, sincere, idealistic people, spanning the patient centuries, who pray, worship and labor for peace and good will among men, only to find that the violence of war and evil-doing increases and flourishes. It is an old and honorable piece of knowledge that the more you fight a thing the more life you give it. Those who study and understand Quimby will know why. It is the principle of "mind on mind," and "man acts as he is acted upon."

Freud taught us about compulsions but largely in the negative sense—that our unresolved fears govern us above and beyond our conscious choices. Again, Paul had anticipated the complete picture and had given the answer to the problem of all the ages: "Know ye not, that to whom ye yield yourselves servants to obey [what you mentally attend to], his servants ye are. . . . whether of sin unto death, or of obedience unto righteousness." *Romans 6*

In modern words, all our actions are the conditioned reflexes of that to which we have consistently offered our minds and this is a way of bondage and servitude until we learn what binds us and then the jig is up. Now we are no longer compelled by error, but with equal force, unalterably compelled by truth. Or, as Paul says it: "But now being made free from sin, and become servants to God, ye have your fruit unto holiness, and the end everlasting life." *Romans 6*

The way to mastery is always through servantship. Those who seek preferment rather than excellence are doomed to fail from the beginning. Those who are meek and lowly of heart (amenable to teaching) will waken one morning to be clothed in the robes of mastership.

So Quimby is now measuring the workings of mind and coming up with his own unique definition: *Mind is spiritual matter.* Had it followed Liebault and Bernheim, western psychology might have drawn closer to that stream of light that came through the window that Lucius had opened. But their mind-set prevented it. In these pages we shall keep on looking through that window.

The ancient Greek learned about his own emotions as a play of Sophocles unfolded on the stage before him. He saw himself revealed in the action of the play. Quimby learned of the tremendous spiritual powers of humanity by watching Lucius and others in the mesmerized state. As he watched, his understanding underwent a dramatic change; he "rose from the dead" and entered into an entirely new kind of life, the "dead" being those who were oblivious to the powers and wonders of the spiritual world in which they lived.

The great medical psychologists and hypnotists, from the contemporary Braid to the latter day Freud, had witnessed most of the same phenomena, but they did not see the light streaming through that window of Lucius. Only Quimby saw, understood and put it into practice. The Nancy School in France is credited with the discovery that "the subjective mind is constantly amenable to suggestion." One, writing in 1930 says: "Bound to no theory and working alone, Quimby reached conclusions as to the suggestibility of the human mind some ten years prior to the announcement of the same conclusions by Professor Liebault, who preceded and founded the Nancy School of hypnotism.   He not only reached them and put them into practice, but he went further along the broad highway of modern psychology than any man of his day." (Fleta Campbell Springer, *According to the Flesh*, New York, Coward-McCann, Inc.). He is still far out in front. Let's see if we can follow him.

In his first experiment, described in the last chapter, he saw his own secret thoughts dramatically acted out by Lucius. He saw that mind in the mesmerized state was more amenable to other minds in the vicinity. He had already seen this in part or at least suspected it, when in his early days with Lucius he had him diagnose disease and prescribe for it. On one occasion Lucius had prescribed a simple herb tea; the doctor in attendance had administered the tea and the patient got well. Since the doctor had previously administered this tea and the patient had not improved, Quimby reasoned that if the tea were of value in one case it would have been also in the other. He reasoned that Lucius was reading the doctor's mind. He found that people were much more likely to "*believe a man with his eyes closed than one with his eyes open.*" Whenever Lucius prescribed a medicine, it was more effective.   From experiments and events like this,

Quimby developed his theory that "*our minds mingle.*" We live in a psychic sea of other men's thoughts. Influences, good and bad, are all around us. This gave rise to the old proverb that "the dead rule." Most of us are walking around with habits from the stone-age, with opinions and beliefs that are, in William Blake's words, "mind-forged manacles."

Then began Quimby's controlled experiments. After this incident (of getting and replacing the hat), he never gave Lucius a verbal command or request. Neither Lucius nor anyone else could know Quimby's intentions. This was the beginning of his science.

> *At first I found that my own thoughts affected the subject, and not only my thoughts but my belief. . . .if I believed anything, the effect would follow whether I was thinking of it or not. . . .my object was to discover what a belief was made of and what thought was. This I found out by thinking of something my subject could describe, so that I knew that he must see or get the information from me in some way.*

At this point Quimby tested this principle exhaustively by imaging all sorts of objects and creatures, which Lucius described and reacted to. If Quimby imaged a bear, Lucius recoiled in fear and it did not allay the fear to be told that the bear was only a mental image. Quimby was slowly but surely discoveing the Other Self with its tremendous powers. He is finding that "*ideas take form*" and "*man has the power of creation.*" He is discovering the Deep Self in man which speaks in the Bible: "Ask me of things to come and concerning the works of my hands, command ye me." He is searching for and finding the nature of mind and redefining it as "*spiritual matter*" because it is constantly changing under the influence of oneself and others. Therefore it is not intelligent in the sense that it can choose and initiate. It is rather a "*medium for ideas.*" Quimby will observe that the mind of a newborn child is like a blank tablet and everyone and everything in its environment scribbles on it until it is made not in the image of its ideal or its possibility, but rather in the confused imagery of extraneous and sundry ideas.

The behaviorists and determinists have insisted that we are each and all products of external influences but usually have failed to say a word about how those influences work. If there were no mind to react to influences, there could be no influence. It the mind were not receptive to influences, they could have no effect. The story of the prince and the pauper is an old one and ever true. The princeling in a poor environment becomes poor, and the pauper in a good environment is conditioned to act like a prince. Or to paraphrase the thought of the great educator, Loyola: "Give me the child until he is seven and I will make him so strong he will fear nothing or so weak that he will never lift a finger in his own promotion or defense." But if the child is an idiot, his environment and your teaching will make no difference. Where there is no responsive mind, there is no influence from externals. What you know is what you are and if you don't know, there is no experience. That is why the *Book of Beginnings* says that Adam "knew" his wife and from that knowing came all the generations of the earth, for Eve or knowing is the "mother of all living."

> *The world makes mind intelligence. I put no intelligence in it but make it subject to intelligence.*

Quimby's conception of mind has many modern analogies. He compared it to clay which could be fashioned by a potter, to earth in which seeds are sown by wisdom or by error and to mortar used in erecting a building. Today we have various recording devices like the phonograph, the tape recorder, the computer, etc. Take the computer as a good example of how mind as Quimby defines it works. The computer has no intelligence, but it records and memorizes intelligence. When being operated, it is always changing. Information is being erased and more put in. If you put a tape recorder on "record" and let it run it will pick up all the sounds and voices in its vicinity and preserve the hodgepodge. This is how the mind picks up errors and accepts limitation and disease when there is a deficiency of wisdom to guide and control the process. This is also the way the mind records its exposure to health, strength and beauty.

After Quimby was rich in wisdom he observed, "*Let man be made acquainted with his true character and his relations to his fellowman and you will not see so many miserable [people] without friends or money.*" At this point in his own development he is getting acquainted with his own true character. He is meeting The Other Self.

He is observing that man has two identities. One he will call The Scientific Man and the other The Man of Belief. The latter is also called The Man of Opinions as contrasted with truth. He also calls these The Two Brothers and later we shall find many other names such as The Spiritual Man and The Natural Man.

While the great medical hypnotists and psychologists from Braid to Freud were hung up on pathology, physiology and general analysis of the subconscious, Quimby was looking at the light streaming through Lucius' window and was discovering the hidden splendor in man.

Continuing our watch with him, we find him in his early days as a mesmerist often inducing mental anaesthesia so surgeons could operate. Ether had not yet been demonstrated by Dr. William Morton, the Boston dentist, and chloroform would not be used until 1848 in England.

On April 18, 1845, A. T. Wheelock, M.D., of Belfast wrote to the Editor of the Boston Medical and Surgical Journal about a "case of painless surgery for the removal in July, 1844 of a polypus from the nose of a patient in the mesmeric condition: The patient came from Montville, 14 miles distant, to Belfast for the purpose of having me operate. . . .the tumor was of an oblong-rounded form, largely attached base, probably half an inch in its smallest diameter, and had been there three months. The base was larger proportionally than the average of cases within my experience and so firmly adhered, that in removing it I was obliged to tear it away in pieces. I had lain out my instruments and was about proceeding in the operation, when she proposed to be magnetized if it was possible, as she dreaded the pain that would have to be borne; and as she was entirely unacquainted in town, at her request I procured the attendance of a gentleman who had the reputation of being a good magnetizer (Mr. P. P. Quimby) although entirely faithless on my own part, as I told her at the time and others before, who had asked what I thought of animal magnetism. I am quite confi-dent that the lady and Mr. Quimby had never met before, and that there was nothing previously concerted. I am also confident that she took no medicine to induce stupor. In ten minutes after commencing, she was put into a state of apparently natural sleep, sitting upright in her chair, breathing and pulse natural—color of countenance unchanged.   We then moved her from the back part of my room where she happened to be sitting to a window for light. Mr. Quimby then asked her if she felt well. She answered distinctly, 'yes.' I immediately (in the presence of several of our most noted citizens who had been called at their own request) began to remove the polypus and did it thoroughly, scraping the sides of the nostrils repeatedly with the forceps so as to be sure that I had removed all of the remaining fragments. There was some hemorrhage, say nearly an ounce of blood. I was operating four or five minutes at least. During the whole time she evinced not the slightest symptom of pain, either by any groaning, sighing or motions whatever, but was in all respects precisely like the dead body. I felt convinced that I might as well have amputated her arm. The circumstances that struck me at the time most singularly of all was this: as soon as the blood began to run down the fauces, there was a slight, rough, rattling sound of the breathing. One of the bystanders said 'she is choking to death.' Mr. Quimby hawked and spit repeatedly, when she did the same, and spit the blood out of her mouth. In about ten minutes after, she was awaked, but said that she was unconscious that anything had been done, complained of no pain, and found that she could now breathe freely through her nose, that had been entirely closed up for several preceding months."

In Quimby's *Lecture Notes*, so-called by Dresser, (*The Quimby Manuscripts*, Edited by Horatio W. Dresser, The Julian Press, New York, 1961) and in the Journal kept by Lucius, we can trace the progressive conclusions drawn by Quimby from these early mesmeric experiences. It is now well known that a special relationship exists between operator and subject. They are as one. Even to the cadence of the breathing. Very early, Quimby discovered that the first step in mesmerizing was to get and hold the attention of his subject. When the subject passed into the mesmerized state, the ordinary faculties such as seeing, reasoning, judging, willing, etc., were suspended and his non-reasoning Deep Mind was responsive to Quimby. Thus what Quimby saw, the subject saw and what Quimby felt, the subject felt. Thus when the blood seemed to be choking the patient, "Mr. Quimby hawked and spit repeatedly, when she did the same, and spit the blood out of her mouth."

> . . . .*all persons who have ever tried any experiments in mesmerism know that the subject is very sensitive and*

*will taste or smell what the mesmerizer
does. . . .the fluids equalize in the
mesmerizer and the mesmerized and
their taste is as one, precisely as two
instruments are brought to accord with
one another by the performer. On this
principle diseases are conveyed from
one to another.*

*Now as these fluids are under the
control of the mind, it is very necessary
that a person should know how to
govern them, so that they shall not get
the mastery of the mind and bring the
persons into the same state that Paul
was in when he said that the spirit
warreth against the flesh. . . .*

Perhaps it was another early case of surgery
with himself as the mental anesthetist that gave
him this insight into the special relationship
existing between operator and subject:

*I was sitting by a patient whom I had
put to sleep that she might have a
needle extracted from her arm, and
while the surgeon was performing the
operation, she said to me, "Does it not*

> *hurt you?" I replied, "No." She said, "I should think it would."   Here was a person awake to all that was going on,who at the same time took my body and arm for the one in which the needle was. When I mesmerized my subject, if his nose itched, he would say to me, "I wish you would scratch your nose," and if I did it would satisfy him.*

Here in these early writings is Quimby, the inventor, the watch and clock maker, schooled and experienced in making wheels and springs and weights and calculating and building into every minute part the mathematical accuracy that will tell the time. But now he is leaving one world and going into another, and the inquiring, inventive mind that has always been interested in investigating every new thing is absorbed in the new phenomena of mesmerism and will shortly be known as one of the best mesmerists in the state. For those of us who know him a century and a quarter later only by his writings and his deeds, he is also the modern world's first psychoanalyst and also the first modern semanticist; for as early as this period we are here discussing, he took issue with the savants of the French Committee that investigated mesmerism over the use of the word imagination. For the rest of his life he was at pains to show how faulty was language as a means of communicating because people assigned differing meanings to words. The story of Babel is not merely a historical event but a description of the ordinary mind of humanity. When one says "brick," another understands "straw."

We are used to observing that there is an inner splendor in man or we speak of the God within. Quimby took such expressions out of the realm of theory and mystery and demonstrated the facts openly and practically. We don't know exactly what his immediate reaction was when he first saw human flesh cut and carved by the surgeon's scalpel, and there was no pain. Surely he was impressed. Surely he must have felt somewhat like Jacob of old when he dreamed of a ladder connecting heaven and earth and awoke and exclaimed: "Surely the Lord is in this place and I knew it not. . . .this is none other than the house of God and this is the gate of heaven." (Genesis 28) But Quimby was not content to marvel and wonder. He wanted to know and he wanted to know why and how. The world was full enough of opinions and beliefs.

For four exciting years with Lucius and others, Quimby carried on these experiments in mesmerism and witnessed the amazing results. On one occasion the 19 year old Lucius records in his journal: "Quimby has been doing miracles. He has cured a man that could not walk nor speak." We know from his *Lecture Notes* that he "talked" with the deaf and dumb and restored the insane.   Moreover, he knew how he did it and therefore he called his method a science.

> *It is in insanity as in other diseases, necessary to make an impression more powerful than that which preceded this diseased state and thus lead or drive the mind into a new channel of thought.*

Having discarded what was in the books because "*man had begun to philosophize before he understood anything about the subject he was trying to teach others.*"   he pioneered another course.

> *I had arrived at the point when my subject could read the thoughts of persons and could travel and explain what the persons knew and also see*

and describe what anyone else in the room knew.

By "travel" he means mental travel as when he mesmerized Lucius and sent him to a distant place or a ship at sea.

> *During the winter of 1843 I visited Wiscasset with my subject and lectured before an audience and gave experiments illustrating my theory of mesmerism. After putting my subject into a clairvoyant state, a gentleman by the name of Clark was placed in communication with him.* [an operator can transfer control to another.]   *Mr. Clark directed him to find the Bark. . . . on board of which was his son.   He immediately saw the bark, described the vessel minutely, gave a general description of the Captain, Mate and his son—asked the Captain what time he would arrive in New York, and received the answer, which he communicated to Mr. Clark in the presence of the whole audience.*

Among a number of newspaper clippings still

preserved among *The Quimby Papers*, saved these many years by George Quimby, son of Phinneas, is one from the Wiscasset paper detailing this event and especially the mail's confirmation of all that Lucius had seen and heard. This is an example of clairvoyance or double sight or as modern investigators call it, "remote viewing."

Here are some singular insights coming through Lucius' window: There is a level of mind variously called the magnetic state, the excited state, the subconscious, clairvoyance, the Subliminal, the Deep Self, etc., in which all things are present.

> *Time and space, distance and matter
> are no impediments to its action. Give
> it direction towards any subject and
> everything connected with it is present.*

He had discovered the Omnipresence, the realm where everything is in the eternal now, eternity or timeless time. Think of anything or anyone, past or present or to come, and it is present now. Thus Lucius, under Quimby's prompting, could follow a dead man and be with him in Ohio, could go to a ship at sea and converse with the Captain, ask him a question and get the answer, go to any place or scene and describe it accurately. All of which taught Quimby that this Clairvoyant Self or Other Mind or Deep Self sees without eyes, hears without ears and can in all ways act independently of the ordinary mind or the natural man. This he saw was the "Christ in you, the hope of Glory." And because this Christ is in one, he or she can do all things through "Christ which strengtheneth me."

Now the clockmaker, who had once thought of man as a machine, operated by unknown forces, saw the operator of the machine—a wisdom he had long ago set out in search of.

> *I made sail for what was uppermost in my mind, to see if there was any wisdom outside of what we call man.*

Let the reader think for a moment of that Other Self that is beyond pain, can go anywhere, see anything, ask questions and get answers and information without the one being questioned being aware he has answered. Think of the surgical operations without pain, for example. Before ether or chloroform, the mortality of patients after surgery averaged 29 percent in a well-run hospital and rose to as high as 50 percent . Even after ether (1847), the rate went from 29 percent to 23 percent . But in Bengal, India, a Scottish M.D., by the name of James Esdaille performed more than 300 major operations with mental anaesthesia alone. These included amputation of limbs, removal of breasts, cataracts, wens and tumors in throat and mouth. His Indian patients felt no pain and what is more, they survived. There were no deaths on the table. The mortality from post-operative infection was 5 percent . All this in a day when surgeons went from dissecting a dead body to the maternity ward without washing. Louis Pasteur was years away from showing the damage of bacteria and Lister was a boy.

How did Esdaille do it? By Mesmerism. He put his patients asleep. Orderlies took turns making passes while a leg was amputated or a 40 pound tumor was removed. Stitched up and taken back to his room, the patient felt no pain and did not know what had happened. And there was no infection in a day when infection was rampant!

If this touches the springs of wonder and awe in one, then he knows what the psalmist meant: "I am fearfully and wonderfully made." His experiences surely made Quimby wonder and marvel and change. Having been in the light, how could he ever be in the dark again?

"*Then I became a medium myself,*" and the ladder by which he climbed to this enlightenment was discarded. Lucius had helped him know himself and mesmerism had been his tool. But as in the beginning, he would still affirm that "*a complete knowledge of mesmerism is necessary to a good understanding of the practical art of our science.*"

Now, what light do we see streaming through the window that Lucius has opened in 1843? The great medical doctors who experimented with hypnosis found the same phenomena that Quimby found, but they did not see the splendor. They were "dead" in their own mind-set. The Bible reports the birth of the Saviour as a time of deliverance and great joy for all people. But the language is of parable and symbol: in a manger at Bethlehem, in the city of David, a virgin and the angels, etc. What Quimby learned by diligent labor and patient experiment is all there in that revered announcement. But, as with those on the way to Emmauas, (Luke 24) how can we understand except someone explain the scriptures? Quimby did just that, not by direct study of the scriptures, but by scientific experiment with the double consciousness: being in two places at once, taking the feeling of the sick, etc. Because so many of his patients were sick from their religious beliefs, he had to concern himself with these beliefs.

> *The question is often asked, why I talk about religion and quote scripture while I heal the sick. My answer is that sickness being what follows a belief, and all beliefs containing disease, the belief contains the evil which I must correct. . . .one-half of the diseases of man arise from a false belief in the Bible.*

With his new insight he could see through the symbol and the parable. They were talking about what he, himself, was experiencing: with the discovery of the Subliminal Self, the world is new, time (the calendar) begins anew, man is reborn. The coming to consciousness of this Self is the birth of Christ. He who sees without eyes, hears without ears, can smell and taste and touch and feel without the senses of the physical body, who has other amazing faculties, who can take up serpents and if he drink any deadly thing, is unhurt, who can pass through fire and not be burned, through the water and not be drowned, who is above pain; birthless and deathless, transcendent and free—this is the "more light" which came through the window of Lucius. Park Quimby, the pragmatist, never content to philosophize only, saw this, explained it and demonstrated it, like the true scientist he was.

> *As facts are what I want to get at, I take my own way to collect them.*

4

In Two Places at Once

The mystics have told us of that Other Place. They have told us how the ecstasy came upon them and the ordinary world was transformed. All things that ever were or ever would be were present now. But they could describe it only in abstractions. Where they had been and how to return they did not know. Note then the simple announcement of one who went there and returned, knew where he had been and how he got there, and could go again at will:

> *I then became a medium myself, but not like my subject. I retained my own consciousness and at the same time took the feelings of my patient. Thus I was able to unlock the secret which has been a mystery to mankind for ages.*

By becoming a medium, he means that now his mind was acutely sensitive to other minds. We are all mediums to some degree. That, as we have seen, is the nature of mind. It is a medium for ideas. It is not intelligence; it is a medium for or a receiver of intelligence. Intelligence means news or information. The intelligence that mind receives is of two general kinds: Truth and Error, Wisdom and Knowledge, Science and Opinion. Sometimes Quimby will confuse some of these terms and the reader will have to follow the text closely to understand what he means.

Not only is each human mind a medium for other minds but it is also a medium for minds which lived years ago. In the experiments with clairvoyance, Quimby found that the attention of Lucius had only to be directed to a person, living or dead, and instantly he, Lucius, was with the person exchanging information with him. Hence it can be a chilling or a cheering remembrance that "our minds mingle." We all live in a kind of psychic sea of thoughts that humans are thinking and thoughts that humans have thought. We are repeaters and our minds, the echoes of dead men's tales. If all people were able to be in two states at once, as Quimby was, we should all be completely honest, for we should have no secrets.

It is a common error to speak of "our ancestral brain" as though we have been handed this half-animal nature to train and manage as best we can. We speak of man and pre-man, the latter a clumsy, hairy sort of brute from whom we descended.   This limits the picture of man.   We are not only animals evolving toward the dignity called man. We are now, in principle, all that we ever shall be. Evolution must be preceded by involution and involution was the word of God. Our hairy forefathers were the inheritors of the whole nature of humanity, both as we know it now and as we dream it will be. We are inheritors of all, both good and bad. Our judgments of good and bad are often erroneous. Good and bad are not in matter, that is in people, places, things and situations, but rather in our thought of them. People become concerned with sins of the body and overlook the real sins which are malice, envy, greed and just plain uncharitableness. Jesus never prescribed rules for conduct. He said, "What is that to thee" and "Go and sin no more." He also said, "Love God and one another." Do you realize that if people did that, they would do no evil? There would be no need for codes of ethics or morality. But humans don't know what good and bad are. When they do, they will have their eyes opened and be as gods, "Knowing good and evil." The whole pilgrimage of man is toward this end. We are not only animals evoluting toward the dignity called man. I repeat, we are now, in principle, all that we ever shall be. Our forefathers were inheritors of all, both good and bad. The way of life is to distinguish truth from error, wisdom from opinion and then let wisdom rule. We are not going anywhere in time. We are travelers in consciousness. "Do not run; it is only to yourself you go." We are also one with all the animals and creatures of every sort. They speak the Language of Silence and we speak it with them. We are all mediums of some kind of psychic input and we are transmitters. Our study is to distinguish between good and evil or wisdom and opinion and to walk humbly with wisdom. Our task is to become a medium of wisdom and to shut the door on opinions.

So we are all mediums; but Quimby was a special and particular kind of medium. Lucius was a medium above the average, for when mesmerized, he passed over to that Other Mind which sees without eyes and hears without ears and has no need of any of the ordinary five senses. But Quimby's achievement was more singular still. He continued using the five senses —natural senses he calls them—but simultaneously was in the Other Place with almost unlimited awareness of the spiritual or invisible world. We can visualize him there in his treatment room, holding the hand of a patient, talking with him or her and at the same time holding a conversation with the unseen real person. This was one way in which he showed that "man has two identities."

> *I found that I had the power of not only feeling their aches and pains, but the state of their mind.*

That is why I have called him the modern world's first psychoanalyst, for he not only felt the pain of his patient, but could trace its origins and describe its growth.   For example, a father brought his daughter to see Dr. Quimby. She had all the appearance of dropsy. As was his custom and manner of treatment, they sat down and he took her by the hand. Soon he had the feeling that they were going off some distance. At last he saw water. It was the ocean and they were on it. Presently he saw a brig in a gale. He also saw a man on the bowsprit, dressed in an oilcloth suit. He fell overboard and the vessel hove to and the the man sank. Here was Quimby in two places at once: in his normal body with two other bodies seated in a room. But his spiritual self which he will call "*the scientific man*" was far away both in time and space. For when he communicated his vision to the patient, she told him that was the way her husband perished five years ago.

> *This was a reality although it happened five years before. Now to cure the lady was to bring her from the scene of her troubles. This I did and she recovered.*

In another place, apparently thinking of this case, he explains that if a person lost a friend at sea, the shock upon his nervous system would disturb the fluids of his body and create around him a vapor like a cloud and "*in this cloud they create the essence of their trouble.*" Recall what he has announced before:

> *I discovered that ideas took form and the patient was affected just according to the impression contained in the idea.*

So the lady had her vapor or cloud and in this cloud was her functioning identity or conception of herself—overwhelming loss, deprivation and sorrow —in this she lived and moved and had her being. To use a frequent expression of his, her senses were attached to this tragedy, that is she had a mental fixation on the tragedy. Because he was so sensitive, he could feel her feelings. That made them psychically one and in that oneness

Quimby made the choice to walk her out of those feelings into other, more happy ones. When he felt that she was anchored in the new feelings, his work was done and the patient was healed of whatever physical disability that had resulted from this mental fixation.

> *This cloud, being a part of their nervous system, acts upon the body. . . .unless the scene can be destroyed, it will destroy the body. . . .now when I sit down with a person I see the spiritual form* [of the person] *in this cloud, like a person driven out of his home. They sometimes appear very much frightened, which is almost always the case with insane persons. I show no disposition to disturb them and at last they approach me cautiously, and if I can govern my own spirit or mind I can govern theirs. At last I commence a conversation with them. They tell me their trouble and offer to carry me spiritually to the place where their trouble commenced.*

So the travels of Lucius now become the travels of Quimby. He no longer goes as a passenger, so to speak, on Lucius' ship but comes and goes at will in scientific fulfillment of the wish of Solomon: "I am but a little child; I know not how to go out or to come in. . . . give therefore thy servant an understanding heart to judge thy people, that I may discern between good and evil." I Kings 3. Solomon asked for wisdom. Quimby asked the same, for long before:

> *I made sail for what was uppermost in my mind: to see if there was any wisdom outside of what we call man.*

He found there was. He found that the mind was not the giant it was fabled to be; it was a medium for wisdom or for error. When wisdom governed it, all went well. When error influenced the mind, man became sick. Now his eyes were open. He could distinguish between good and evil and knew that

> *The distinction between things seen and not seen causes all the controversy of the world for what all agree to there is no controversy about.*

The Bible chapter quoted above also announces that "Solomon loved the Lord." And because of this the Lord was able to teach him wisdom. What you attend to (love) leaves its likeness with you. The same was true of Quimby. After he found what governs human beings, he knew the law or Lord and he loved it. Because he loved the Lord, he was loving. I have never known, heard or read of any more compassionate man than P. P. Quimby. From the time he discovered the law, he began to drop his opinions and beliefs and this made his mind teachable. A vessel that is full can contain no more. He made his vessel empty and opened it to wisdom. For him wisdom was what could be demonstrated and proved. He not only talked about his theory; but he talked it. As we say today, He put his feet where his mouth was.

In addition to sitting with the sick and allowing himself to be conducted to the place of their injury, he went alone in response to letters. The following is good sample of the dozens of letters he wrote to patients:

> *Your letter apprised me of your situation and I went to see if I could affect you. I am still trying to do so but do not know that I can without sitting down and talking with you as I am at*

> *present. So I will sit by you a short time and relieve the pain in your stomach and carry it off. . . .when you read this, I shall be with you: and do as I write. I am in this letter, so remember and look at me. . . .let me know how you get along. If I do not write, I may have time to call,* [spiritually] *for that does not require so much time.*

His assurance to the patient that he will *"relieve the pain in your stomach and carry it off"* recalls the ancient lore about The Messiah: he goes to the underground place of the sick, makes an incision in his side, hides all the diseases of the sick in it and closes it up and then bears them all away into nothingness.

This is exactly what Quimby did. By 1859 he was seeing five hundred patients a year in his Portland offices. Sympathizing with all these and the many who consulted him by mail took its toll, for his zeal and compassion would not allow him to rest and recuperate. On one occasion he sat with a girl subject to fits and nearly had one himself. His son had to be called to take him home where he spent the rest of the day in bed.

Thereafter he would not take cases of this kind.

> *It is not an easy thing to steer the ship of wisdom between the shores of poverty and the rocks of selfishness. If he* [the teacher and healer] *is all self, the sick lose that sympathy which they need at his hand. If he is all sympathy, he ruins his health and becomes a poor outcast on a cold, uncharitable world. For the sick can't help him and the rich won't. It is difficult to steer clear and keep your health.*

So he went on in wisdom unlocking the mysteries of philosophy and wonderment and demonstrating his theory at every step. Wisdom was his passport to the other worlds which we shall consider next.

5
The Two Worlds

In one particular, the civilized man is
still brother to the savage; his thoughts
seldom rise above the dust of which
he is made. – Robert Quillen

To the primitive, "seeing is believing." What
he cannot see, he cannot believe. So he makes
his gods of wood and bronze and clay. To him
these are "real." The civilized man does
something similar. The body and environment
are real to him; the world of thought, choice,
imagination is vague. In order to explain things
and situations he materializes them in his
thought. Thus heaven and hell are places to
which the person goes after the body dies. To
see that this is a materialization in thought of an
abstract spiritual truth, we need only examine the
religious teaching of the race. All believe in an
after state of some kind but only occasionally is it
spoken of as a condition of mind rather than a
physical place. Even then there is no more clarity
of understanding than when a person says glibly,
"It's all in your mind," without fathoming the way in
which that is true. Let us take heed therefore that
the light which is in us be not darkness (Luke
11:35). How can light be darkness? (Luke 11:35)

It cannot in the literal sense. Then, of course the non-literal or figurative sense is meant: your light is the information or knowledge your mind possesses on any subject. If that light is insufficient to see your way clear, then it is dark and the goals of life are obscure. If your light or understanding is unable to comprehend the saying or writing of another, then the light that is in you is dark. You do not see clearly. You will interpret what you hear or read in terms of what you know and that may not be sufficient. Like the old fellow who saw the first steam engine on the track. He asked where the horse was. When told that it ran by steam, that the steam was made inside the boiler etc., he said, "Oh, I see, the horse is inside." In the parables of Jesus, ordinary and common things are used to represent uncommon, spiritual truths; but if the reader's mind never jumped from one side of the parable to the other, he is not increasing his light or understanding. Then the true light "shineth in darkness and the darkness comprehended it not."

For Quimby the light was continually increasing and he saw that people did not think spiritually, but rather literally and materialistically. They spoke of "this world and one to come" and meant physical places. Whereas when Jesus used terms like this he meant something far different. In Jesus' teaching, "this world" is not the earth or the globe but the average mind, the race mind, the mass mind with its ignorance, superstition, false beliefs and fears. The "world" is a psychic sea in which all minds mingle and are influenced one by another. Man is trainable, teachable and suggestible, capable of being influenced by errant and wandering ideas. Because he is capable of being influenced by other minds, he can be destroyed by other minds wittingly or unwittingly. That is why the "world" is called the place of the wicked.

His only protection is in science, knowing the truth about himself and his environment. It is a law in physics and in metaphysics that two things cannot occupy the same place at the same time. If one's dish (mind) is full, nothing else can enter. This is reason enough for the ancient teaching of meditation, contemplation and spiritual exercises to keep the mind free of the wrong influences and ever open to more light or science, as Quimby called it.

> *I, like others, once believed that Jesus came to save man from eternal damnation, and to point out the way to*

> *another world, but my practice with the
> sick has produced an entire change in
> my mind in regard to the subject. If
> any of Jesus' truth lingers in the
> religion of the world it would be seen
> in the sick who are just on the verge of
> another world, as they believe. Yet I
> have learned by sitting with them that
> the religious belief is the worst torment
> one can have at such a time. Although
> they may say that they rejoice and are
> ready to go, they are really afraid and
> show as much joy when I tell them
> they will not die, as a condemned
> criminal feels, when kneeling upon his
> coffin, he hears the word of pardon.*

As always, Quimby was learning from the
sick. He sat with them, sympathized with them,
went with them spiritually to the place of their hurt
and led them back to health and happiness.
Because we humans wear masks and seldom
reveal ourselves, it takes someone like a Quimby
to get behind the mask and converse honestly
with the real person.   There he found that
religious beliefs were not so much a "rock of
ages" as a source of dread, especially this belief
in an after life,   whether a heaven or a hell.   The

instinct to believe in an after life is true — "there must be something more" — but its varied conceptions are often fuzzy. Jesus never taught a literal heaven or a literal hell. When he said that he came from the Father into the world, it means that he or the spiritual identity of human kind came from Wisdom and comes into the mass mind, into the world of error, is subject to all its limitations but is never sullied or diminished by them. Like the water from above, it falls to earth and is mixed with all sorts of substances which befoul it and seem to change it, but it never loses its identity for by distillation it can be recovered in all its purity. Quimby's illustration of this is telling. He compares it to a gold piece dissolved into solution by a galvanic battery and then a reversal of the process and the recovery of the solid piece. Read Isaiah 53 again in the light of this. It is our subjective nature which is "despised and rejected of men." The great sin of the world is its self-will, its worship of the brain and its rejection of that without which not anything is made that is made. "Surely he hath borne our griefs and carried our sorrows" for he registers all our opinions and beliefs, every thought, whether good or bad, and then shows it again to us in physical form and experience. Yet he never censures or warns or preaches. Like a sheep before her shearers, he is dumb and opens not his mouth. How else could we learn? If this Wise One within us warned us every time we were thinking wrong, would we ever know the dreadful and wonderful significance of our own thought?

This is what comes from the Father for it is the Father or source of all livingness. Being rejected, it is still available and returns again and again. "I came forth from the Father, and am come into the world: again I leave the world, and go to the Father." (John 16:28). This is the Christ. Jesus was the name of a man. Christ was in him and Christ is in all men. When the Christ is known and welcomed, then man and God are one in the name, Jesus Christ. So:

> *The world that Jesus came from when he said that he came from his Father is not the Christian's world, but the world of Wisdom. And when he came into this world as it is called, he did not mean this world of matter, called the globe, but the world of opinions or the people's beliefs.*

A knowledge of this is part of what Quimby calls "science," as opposed to beliefs and opinions. One is the natural, habitual world and the other is the spiritual world. Every person contains these two. The Bible teaching is that one must die and the other be brought to life and function. As opinions and error (the natural world) die, truth and science rise or are resurrected. It is this simple truth that has been so grossly materialized in religion's teaching of a literal heaven and a literal hell and in projecting the falsehood that somatic death and resurrection are what is meant.

> *In the wisdom of Jesus the word death means simply the change from brutish ignorance to a higher state of knowledge. . . .the end of error is the end of the world. . . . the introduction of religion based on science is the commencement of the new world. . . . He* [Jesus] *did not labor to save men from another world but from the evils of this world.*

To Quimby the trouble with mankind is that *"they are spiritually sick."* To be spiritually well is to enjoy your own thoughts and to move joyously in your feelings about life. So if the end of error is the end of the world, we have died many times.

Where is the five year-old we once were? The ten-year-old? Think back to the time before you were proficient in the job you now do. Where is that mind of ignorance you once were? All dead, but you are here. People often argue about the doctrine of reincarnation but this much is obviously true: each of us dies and is reborn many times within one lifetime. And the law of cause and effect holds true throughout.

Part of being spiritually healthy is to understand that the word "death" does not refer to the body only. The mind too dies and is reborn. But it may be reborn into an equally limiting belief or opinion. When the scripture urges man to be born again, it means it in a very special sense. Not merely change of opinion and viewpoint. Not just emotional change. Not only a change of heart. But an exchange of the wisdom of the world for the wisdom of the spiritual and mental truths which place man above and outside of matter, free of disease and going from strength to strength and from joy to joy. Quimby discovered what religion has confused, that Christ and Jesus are not the same. Jesus was the man and Christ was what he knew and practiced. Christ is synonymous with Truth. Christ is in the world but the world knows it not. It is a mystery. But it knows there is something bigger than man and that at times it breaks through and is known for brief instants. It is the God in man. When Quimby learned to take the feelings of the sick, he was being born into a dimension of Christ. When any great truth is discovered and put into practice for the good of mankind, that is a Christ and a Saviour, saving people from their sins or errors of the past. For example, in Quimby's day, the telegraph was a Christ, "having a spiritual and a natural body." Its spiritual body was not known and not visible until it was demonstrated and then it became a material body. The Christ feeds the multitude with its body and those who understand or drink its blood, live on it. This is often a difficult concept to grasp and to teach for it is clothed about with so much religious jargon and misinformation. One of Quimby's many nautical illustrations will help. Suppose a man wants to be a navigator but knows nothing of the science. He goes to someone who will teach him. He becomes an apprentice and gives his mind to instruction. After a while he becomes proficient and is now a navigator. He has died to his ignorance and risen in his new knowledge and skill. Quimby sees Christ, Truth, Science and the Son of God as synonymous. The trinity Christians have discussed for centurie is Wisdom or the

Father, Truth, the son, and Science, the practice.

> *I assume Wisdom to be the Father of*
> *all and Science the son of Wisdom*
> *and those of us who know Science or*
> *the Son, know Wisdom or the Father*
> *for Wisdom and Science are one.*

And the practice is the doing. We are told that the son is the one who does the will of his father. The father is the creator; if, therefore, the son creates, he is doing the will of his father. If you are not creating health and happiness, you are not yet the son of your heavenly father but still the son of beliefs and opinions. Death and resurrection are in order.

Sometimes people talk as though this were an easy thing to do, to die to one world and enter a new one, to lose one's old self and discover one's Christ. The birth of Christ is not just a change of mind, like a new idea or an exaltation of consciousness. The birth of Christ is the emergence of the Other Self you have always had but which was submerged by false opinions and misguided beliefs.

The word *Christ* means "Anointed." It is

Anglicized from the Greek from the Hebrew and the transliterated word from Hebrew is Meshak or Messiah. The Messiah is "the one who goes down." This has several senses but the following will be of most help to most people.

The thrust of life is always forward. We have desires and ambitions. But there are many barriers and frustration builds up. Anger, envy and other ugly emotions can follow. It is then when one is at his wit's end that the Christ or the Deep Self or the Subconscious intervenes to help us. Everyone remembers his days in school when he or she wrestled over a problem at night, went to bed frustrated and wakened in the morning with the answer in his head. Many studies have been made that show that this is the basic creative process. When Edison was looking for a wax for his new phonograph records, all the available waxes were either too hard for the engraving needle, or too soft. He set his long-time associate, M. A. Rosanoff, to the task of finding a suitable wax. Rosanoff worked for over a year without results but with dogged persistence. The project was more difficult than he had expected and frustration was building. Then it happened. "On Sunday evening I lay on my couch with a headache, smoking cigarettes. I tried to keep my mind a blank; but after a year or more of being held down to my problem by Edison, I could no longer shut out the waxes, even in my sleep.   And suddenly through headache and daze, I saw the solution. . . .but the first thing next morning I was at my desk and half an hour later I had a record in the softened wax cylinder.   It was the solution!" (*How to Think Creatively,* Hutchison).

Dozens, hundreds of modern discoveries and inventions have come about in just this way, from Kekule's molecular structure ring theory to the Xerox copier.   Investigation has found four stages to the creative process: The first step is desire and an attempt to reach the goal through trial-and-error with growing frustration.   The second step is giving up, exhaustion, renunciation. The conscious mind gives up and the activity becomes subconscious. Then, after sleep, or diversion, the insight or answer comes "like a bolt from the blue."   The scripturers describe it as " a moment when ye think not" and it comes "like a thief in the night." The thief does not announce his coming and in spiritual matters, unlike worldly matters, the thief leaves you richer after his visit for he takes away your frustration and pain.

The wish must be intense, with personal anxiety also, else the function does not reach the creative pitch necessary. The Deep Self must be alerted, called to attention and given the problem by surrender of self- will. That is why suffering is involved.   But it is a creative suffering for a constructive end. "He suffered for the joy that was set before him." The psychology of our era does not lend much support to this insight but it is alive and well in many people in many walks of life.

The ancients understood this process and wrote about it. That is what I see in the account of Jesus being baptized of John. He went down into the Jordan and came up with the blessing. It takes two to tango and without the engagement of the subconscious, things do not happen. Idle wishing is insufficient. The wish or desire must be a cry for help which is driven down into the Deep Self by the energy of wishing.   Then with its computer-like accuracy, it solves the problem and presents the answer "in a moment when ye think not."

So the Christ is that kind of mind which has been anointed by the waters of Wisdom, which has come up from the depths (out of the depths have I cried unto thee – Psalms 130) which has ascended on high, that is, to a place of leadership and rulership in a person.   Quimby learned all this not by a laborious study of esotericism but rather by sitting with the sick and curing them.

> *Take the man Jesus, as a man of flesh and blood like all other men, and give him the knowledge that mind is matter and that matter is under the control of a higher power that can act independently of matter or ideas, and that he, Jesus, could be in two places at the same time and be outside of the body or idea called Jesus, then it would not be very hard to believe that this knowledge called Christ, which Jesus had, should say, Although you destroy this idea of Jesus, he that is Christ should rise or make himself known to the people. For this Christ or Truth had the power to assume any form that it pleased and as the people knew it not except as it came within their senses as the natural man, they could not believe till it took the form the people called Jesus, t herefore the report went out that Jesus rose from*

the dead. . . .

For Jesus never believed nor tried to prove that their idea of Jesus should rise, but that this Christ or Wisdom would take to itself a body to prove to them that man lives when the world calls him dead and a knowledge of this is the other world.

"And I give unto them eternal life" (John 10). What is this eternal life? A place beyond the stars or a state of mind that is at peace? It is difficult for anyone to leave behind the impression of place and locality. It has been with us a long time. The tomb of the ancient Phoenician king bears the words: "His abode eternity." So did every generation of man wish and hope and religiously predict. But the path to eternity is not through bodily death but through the kind of mental and philosophical death we have described in these pages.

Consider this for a start: Water is wet. It runs downhill. It boils at 212 degrees and freezes at 32. Hot air rises. Men walked on the moon because the orbits of earth and moon are constant.

There is a constancy in all nature. There is no caprice. As Professor Hepner of Colgate said it: "On earth, life occurs where the average—as distinct from the range—of the annual temperature is between 32 and 104 degrees Fahrenheit. A drop of forty degrees in the average and another Ice Age would freeze us; a further forty degrees drop and life would be completely extinguished! A similar change of temperature in the opposite direction, lifting the average to, say, 160 degrees, would make life on earth equally impossible. Fortunately for us, the orbit of the earth is unchanging. The universe functions in a remarkably reliable manner, so unvarying that astronomers can set their watches by the surface markings visible on the planet Mars during its rotations," Now, add to such truths as this, Quimby's discovery that disease is not an independent something and you attain to a sublime perspective which gives you spiritual freedom, where you dwell above and beyond the damps and sorrows of this world. This is eternal life, life without change and caprice. This is possible for man only when his mind is directed by Wisdom. Wisdom is God. "Get Wisdom. . . Forsake her not, and she shall preserve thee: love her and she shall keep thee." (Proverbs 4) Only Wisdom is eternal. Only Truth is forever.

Opinion and belief are always changing, ceaselessly in flux. Wisdom is life without birth or death.

6

Walking Past the Graveyard

It is still hard for men to get along with God for thinking of death not as they do. – Mary Austin.

Quimby got along well with God or wisdom, as he called it, for he thought of death not as others do.

> By a mesmerized subject I can prove that there is no death as it is understood by all Christians.

The mesmerized person seems dead and insensate. Prick his finger and it does not bleed. Cut his flesh and he feels no pain. Burn him and he does not flinch. Speak to him and he is unreplying, except to the operator who placed him in this state. "He can fly, walk, do feats of strength, pass into the sea and describe things lost." He can find and give information that he knows nothing of in his ordinary mind.

Quimby became so acquainted with this mesmerized self and its superior spiritual powers that it took away all fear of death. It proved to him that an individual can act with all his usual faculties entirely independent of the body. He saw that there is another self, a superior self, that does not die with the body because it is not dependent upon the body. People often speak with some pride about "our enlarged brain" as though it were the doer and maker. But the brain dies with the body and then there is an end to all learning. This Other Self can read, write, speak and direct the body even when the latter is weakest. These experiments also proved to Quimby that each mind lives and operates under a belief of opinion, that this belief is like a mesmerizer to a mesmerized person. It controls and directs him but he does not know it. Like the alcoholic, he often proclaims his independence; meanwhile his friends see how he is bound. Quimby found that: "The priest and the physician stand to society as the mesmerizer to his subject." They make beliefs in people and those beliefs put them in bondage.

> *From what I have seen and felt of the mind, I am satisfied that nine tenths of all the old, chronic diseases are the result of wrong impressions produced on the minds of persons by physicians ignorantly, for I do not want to accuse them of knowingly being the authors of so much misery.*

This brings up a point which psychology has omitted. A good belief is just as compulsive as a bad one. Both are beliefs enthroned, and both are the result of "mind on mind." When a person attains faith in his Deep Self, he drops his opinions of limitation and weakness and the spiritual or scientific self becomes more dominantly directive. He is now under good compulsions. His scientific man becomes his mesmerizer and directs, guides and even compels him into the paths of health and happiness. A person can so think that he induces this constructive control and guidance and takes God for his mesmerizer and we say that everything he does is in divine order. Such a person reverses Paul's plight; forces that once worked against him now work for him. Such a person makes his own "luck." Throw him in the water and he will come up with a fish in his mouth.

> *Let a man be made acquainted with his true character and his relationship to his fellowman and you will not see so many miserable, without friends or money.*

How do we live and how do we die? We live

in our beliefs. We have seen how "to believe a thing is to make it."   An old hypnotic demonstration is to tell a hypnotized person to take a seat and indicate a seat already occupied by another person. Without questioning, the hypnotized one will sit down in the lap of the person in the chair. To him the chair is empty because he has been told so. The Deep Self never reasons or debates. It accepts whatever it is told and acts immediately. Also, it can think of only one thing at a time. The subconscious has been called a tumpty-tum mind. That is, it likes a rut. Thus if told to be seated it assumes an empty chair and acts accordingly. The person is "living in his belief." Our life is our belief. To those who are looking on, the scene is ludicrous and irrational, but to the hypnotised person, all is perfectly natural and normal.   That is why a limiting belief can be a grave and to get out of it is a resurrection. To Quimby this was the teaching of Jesus.

> *Jesus admitted the two worlds not as places but as conditions of mind . . . . Jesus never believed or tried to prove that their idea of Jesus should rise, but that this Christ or Wisdom would take to itself a body to prove* [that] *man lives*

*when the world calls him dead, and a
knowledge of this is the other world . . .
. the world of opinions is the old world,
the world of science is the new world.*

To attain to this new world "ye must be born
again." To many this is a conundrum just as it
was to Nicodemus in the Bible where the
statement is found (John 3): "How can a man be
born when he is old? Can he enter the second
time into his mother's womb, and be born?"
Jesus explains to him that a person must be born
of Water (or flesh, because all bodies are born in
or from a bag of water) and of the spirit. The spirit
is the immaterial side of life and the only
immaterial thing we know about man is mind and
thought.   Every one of us has been born of
water. The next birth awaiting us is the birth of a
new mind.   "Be renewed in the spirit of your
mind." The spirit of your mind is the way your
thoughts make you feel. If you are down a lot, you
are dispirited. If you are hyperactive, impulsive
and a bundle of unexpended energy, you are
high-spirited. The mind that is down is thinking
the wrong ideas. So to renew the spirit of the
mind is to engage the mind with Truth instead of
error. Part of that exercise is to increase the
understanding that we are not our body; therefore

what happens to the body at its death is not crucial. The body is our instrument to manifest our thought. Paul speaks of its death in this way: "Thou sowest not that body that shall be, but bare grain, it may chance of wheat, or some other grain: (the seed that is sown disappears and a new seed or seeds appear). But God giveth it a body as it hath pleased him, and to every seed his own body." To quote myself in another writing: "We are the seed of God and we have been planted in the earth. As the plant puts out a display of stems and leaves and blossoms, so we put forth a display of arms and legs and brain in order to gain experience through matter. We are stimulated by and react to our environment and out of these sensations we acquire discernment and understanding. We 'sow' or expend, through exercise and work a physical body. We frolic in sensation and   for a time are deep in the earth but throughout it all a backward process of involution is going on in consciousness.

Just as in the growth of a flowering plant, the original charge of life in the seed or bulb initiates the growth process. But not all of the energy goes into the growing process to produce leaves and blossoms. Some of it is reserved for seed production.   This is what the Chinese call the backward movement of life. Not all of the energy of the growing plant is used in the current manifestation. Some of that energy 'dies' back into forming a seed or bulb. And so it is with you and me. We are dying daily. We are dying while we are living. The living process is apparent. The dying process is less so.

All this feverish activity which we call our life, all this going and coming and doing, acting and reacting is but the outer display. Inwardly, another kind of process is going on: it is the opening of the inner senses and the awakening of spiritual realizations. It is the accumulation of soul content, ready, presumably for another expression. So 'we sow not the body that shall be.' We sow sensation and reap awareness. We sow perception and store up apperception. This gives us a new identity above and beyond the beings wholly transcendent of time and space. In terms of our true self, we are not born and we shall never cease to be. This means that we are now in eternity, the life that does not change. Through a thousand experiences we put on change and variety like the flowering fields, but ever remain more than our display and grander than our experience." (*How the Dead Rise* by Ervin Seale, THE BUILDER, 1968).

To say it in Quimby's way: We live in our beliefs. So long as we stay in a belief we are in prison or "dead." Beliefs are partial knowledge, so every belief must go down until the person lives in Wisdom. This is the Father's house. "I came forth from the Father and am come into the world; again, I leave the world and go to the Father." (John 16:28).

The average person holds his conscious, objective self as precious above all else. He is loathe to change. He dreads death because he identifies with his body. He does not yet know his Other and Real Self except as a mystery. He sees that when the body dies, the brain dies with it for it is part of the body. He equates brain with mind and honors both as sources of intelligence whereas they are but instruments and reflectors of it. For all of us the ancient call still sounds, "Acquaint now thyself with him and be at peace: thereby good shall come unto thee." (Job 22:21) Become increasingly familiar with the Other Self, the Scientific Man, the Transcendent Person, whom Emerson describes as "never born, will not die at your death, and never knew any of your ills or tribulations."

This was Quimby's study and practice. He

overcame that last enemy, the fear of death. So much so that in the hour before his bodily death, he said to his son:

> *I am more than ever convinced of the truth of my theory. I am perfectly willing for the change myself, but I know that I shall be right here with you, just the same as I've always been. I do not dread the change any more than if I were going on a trip to Philadelphia.*

7

Spiritualism

SPIRITISM (SPIRITUALISM) – the
belief that the spirits of the dead
communicate with the living through
the agency of a medium or psychic. –
Columbia Encyclopedia, 2nd Ed.

We have observed earlier in these pages that
everyone is a medium. Every human mind is a
blank to be written on or spoken to by invisibles,
which invisibles are ideas. The devils who
agitate us or the saints who guard us are, in the
last analysis, but ideas which have engaged our
fancy and imagery and led to our conviction. But
when we do not realize this, we project what we
feel but do not know, onto fantasms, ghosts,
goblins and spirits. Then, because we create
what we believe, we see "the spirits."

Thus it was, in 1847, when Quimby was
finishing his experiments in mesmerism, that
there arose what was called the "Rochester
Rappings." In the Fox family, recently removed
from Ontario to upper New York State, were three
daughters: Margaret, Katherine and Leah. They
claimed to have established communication with
the spirit world by means of rappings. They

toured North America and Europe, and in their wake arose great excitement and conviction that at last there was tangible evidence of immortality and that now people had a way of communicating with friends and loved ones who had "gone before." So fast did the awareness of the "Rochester Rappings " spread, that an authority on the phenomena was saying in 1897: "there are millions of stricken hearts whose wounds have been healed by the consolation offered by that conviction."

Spiritualism became the latest parlour game. As far back as 1778, Mesmer had electrified Paris with his cures. In England and America interest in this strange influence called magnetism was aroused. In the smallest communities the subject was talked and retalked and argued and discussed. As Quimby would say, "Ideas are sown in the mind" and fads and crazes arise. Now, instead of trying to magnetize each other, people were falling into trances, and receiving messages from the dead. Mediums appeared everywhere.

Of course there were skeptics and P. P. Quimby was one. Not about the phenomena of spiritualism — he had seen it all before under the

name of mesmerism—but about the alleged
cause. He believed that the medium "tells us our
own thoughts." Just as the mesmerized subject
reports the thoughts of those around him, or to
whom he is directed, so the spiritualistic medium
reports the contents of the minds around him.
Once again he saw the action of "mind on mind."
The medium can report only what is present in the
mind of someone at hand.

> *I will here explain what seems to be a
> mystery to most people, that is: how a
> medium tells us our own thoughts.
> You are sitting at a table with a
> medium and you ask if any spirit is
> present. The answer comes: "Yes,
> your father." You say at once: "That is
> not correct, my father is not dead." The
> spirit contends he is. You ask when
> he died, of what disease, etc.,
> receiving answers which are correct.
> All that was unknown to the medium or
> present company.*

But it was known to your own subjective entity
or Deep Self. The Deep Self or what Quimby
called the Scientific Man, has apparently perfect
memory. On the other hand, the conscious or

objective self has imperfect memory. Therefore you cannot fool the spirits. Your Deep Self constantly announces all that you know of your father and a good medium can pick it up.

> *I know also, if you have a trouble in your body or mind, that I can get the fact from you without your knowing it. . .I know that if you go out of my natural eyes and have a desire that I should come to you, that I can. . . .I know that I can go to a distance and act upon a person and know that I am there and I can make an impression upon a person so strong that the person will be aware of my presence. This is wisdom* [Not belief].

All the phenomena of spiritualism were known to Quimby but he explained them differently. Always the scientist, he was impatient with beliefs and theories which could not be proved. He went to seances with his friends and participated in good will and always came away assured that a large proportion of the converts to spiritualism "are honest, but mislead, for want of some better proof." He admitted that the spirits rapped and tapped and wrote and gave forth amazing information but insisted that these spiritualistic phenomena were similar to those experienced in mesmerism and when people do not realize that these occurrences are the creation of ourselves or some other person, then our superstition calls them, "spirits."

After all, what is a spirit? It is not substance, but shadow. It is not material but immaterial. What is immaterial? Mind or thought. The reader will recall that Quimby would mentally create animals, flowers, fruits and other objects while Lucius was in the mesmerized state and Lucius would see them as real. It made no difference when he was told that these animals were images or shadows. To him they were real. And thus was anticipated what psychology later discovered, that the subconscious mind does not differentiate between a physical image (one seen by the eyes) and one seen inside the mind. So he went on, acknowledging the phenomena of spiritualism but not attributing them to the dead but rather to the minds of the living.

To show the similarity between the experiments then and now under the name of spiritualism, I will relate one or two of the many experiments I used to show.

He tells how he used to put Lucius into the clairvoyant state and then request the audience to give him the name of some individual, whether dead or alive, and Lucius would find him. When a name was handed to him, Quimby passed it to Lucius "who was sitting blindfolded by the committee."

Remember that he had already discovered thought-reading and how minds mingle so –

> *My mode was to make him ask questions, so that the audience would lead him along* [with images and ideas in their minds]. *So I said, Enquire who he is, a man or boy? He said, A man. Is he married? Yes. Tell me if he has any children, and how many? He said he had a wife and three children. Well, find him. He said he left town between two days. Well, find him.*

So he traced the man (John Brown) to Boston, and by enquiring, he followed him to New York and found him in a cooper's shop. Quimby reports that all of this was literally true and suggests that the audience knew the facts, but neither he nor Lucius knew anything of them.

Well, what became of the man? He [Lucius] *said he was dead. Well, said I, find him and bring him here. Said he, He is here. Can't you see him? I then reminded him that he was mesmerized, for in that state everything was as real as in the waking state. So I said, Give a description. Now these descriptions amount to nothing for everyone will make it fit their case. So I said, I don't want that* [a general description]. *If there is anything peculiar about the man, describe it. There is one thing peculiar, he said: this man has a harelip. This was the fact. I asked that question so that if there was anything peculiar the audience would create it.*

Those early experiments convinced Quimby *"that man has the power of creating ideas and making them so dense that they could be seen by a mesmerized subject."*

This also showed him that *"man has an unconscious power that is not admitted which governs his acts."* The natural senses of the average person do not recognize this unconscious power and therefore account for its acts by some superstition or belief. Take the case of the man with the hare lip whom Lucius followed spiritually or mentally or "in the spirit" and found. The people in the audience had a variety of views and explanations. Those who believed that the spirits of the dead return, believed that the man's spirit returned on that evening and that Lucius spoke with him. Some believed it was the work of the devil. Some thought it was collusion. So each person saw the events through and by his own belief. The reader will recall what we said about the hypnotized man taking a seat already occupied. To him the seat is empty because he has been told so. He is operating under his belief and all his experience is in accordance with that belief. Likewise, each member of the audience viewed the events of the evening through his own particular bias or belief.

> *Now I have seen the experiments of spiritualism and I know that they are the workings of Man's belief, and I have proved it to the medium. I knew a medium, very excitable and very susceptible to manifestations, and I tried some experiments on her. I told*

her I would convince her it was her own belief that governed the raps. So when the spirits came, I asked certain questions that I knew she did not agree with me on, neither did any of the company.

For example, Quimby asked the spirits, if he could be in two places at once and if he could make himself known to certain individuals without their knowledge. The spirits denied that he could do this. Then he explained to the company present how he could do these things *"and I know I changed their minds."*

After three or four days there was another gethering or seance with the same people present and Quimby announced that *"now I will convince you that I was right."*

They all laughed and I sat down by the table. The raps came. The question was asked if the spirits were present and the rap answered, Yes. I then repeated what I said [at the previous session] *– can I be in two places at once, etc.*

This time the table rapped that Quimby was right in every one of his questions. When he asked the spirits why they had given one set of answers before and entirely different answers now, they announced that they had been mistaken. Anyone who knows anything about the workings of the subconscious mind knows that it will rationalize any strange conduct and pretend that all is well and right, just as the hypnotized person takes a seat on the lap of another and acts as though all is normal.

But Quimby, the scientist, sees what is happening in all of this.

> *Now this is the case.   As people become educated, the ideas change; this keeps the mind all the time excited.   In a short time, the superstition or fear will change, and the phenomena of today will all cease, and a new phase will spring up, just according to the wisdom* [beliefs] *of the world.*

He had educated that   small group into another belief and operating under and through that belief they had found spirits to confirm it.

Once again he had demonstrated scientifically how the chief belief of the mind governs its individual experience. This is the fundamental in Jesus' teaching: "As thou hast believed, so be it done unto thee." Or, "According to thy faith, so be it done unto thee". The human mind creates nothing but the reflection of its belief. Every person's experience is the projection of his educated mind, whatever the nature of the education.

How often we hear or read of a person who kills because God or the spirits has ordered him or her to do so. Quimby cites one such case of a young widow:

> *I went to see a lady who had cut her throat under the direction of the spirits; she had become insane and was told to kill two of her children.*

She thought he came to kill her but he succeeded in "restoring her to her reason" and convinced her that what she saw and heard was the effect of her own mind.

> *She understood it and the understanding was the cure.*

Quimby, throughout the writing, says that *"the explanation is the cure."* Here he says that the understanding was the cure. Jesus, in the same kind of instances, uses the word "faith." "Thy faith hath made thee whole" (Luke 8:48). Not faith in the sense of belief in a religious doctrine nor faith in the sense of assuming and trusting without evidence or reason but faith as a mental position based upon realization and understanding of basic principles and laws. All these words, as used here (explanation, understanding and faith) are roughly synonymous. We are all on the journey to this new mind and that is why all journeys end within, at home in the Father's house, for the Father's house is Wisdom. Thus, when Quimby brought the woman away from her delusion and fear and showed her that what she saw and heard was the product of her mind under the influence of ideas which she had not understood, he gave her a new mind and this was "faith," a real and present state which is the substance of things to come. The mind creates by projecting its content as onto a screen. All depends on the direction given to the mind. The directing influence can be either truth or error.

Now can any person believe that spirits from the dead came to her persuading her to take the lives of her children? If there is, it is an error of the mind founded upon some false idea, which should be corrected.

We shall deal with his methods of correcting the mind presently, but for now let's look at and think about his terse, pithy assessment of the whole subject of this chapter:

If the spirit is not dead, how can it give an account of what never happened. . .

according to my wisdom man does not die, for so long as he has the belief that he shall die, so long he is not dead but going to die. So when he says through a medium that he is dead, he does not tell the truth, for the very fact of his saying so proves that he is alive.

8

Correcting the Mind

I will now use my skill as far as I am able to correct your mind in regard to your trouble.

We have now come full circle since Chapter I. There we considered that frequently-heard expression of ignorance, "Oh, it's all in your mind," meaning your pain isn't real.

On the contrary, we found that what you feel is real to you. Quimby knew if a patient had a pain because he himself felt the same pain through sympathy. He never denied the pain or called it unreal. What he did deny is that pain or disease existed independently of man and could act on its own. This idea in the mind of man was the great error and needed to be corrected. It is this idea that brings distress to the mind and the distress causes pain.

The mind does not act of itself but "acts as it is acted upon." The mind is acted upon by ideas and only ideas. Things and objects, winds and weather cannot act directly on the mind; they can only suggest certain ideas. The mind is therefore " a medium of ideas." These ideas may be good or bad. A bad idea is a false idea and therefore an error. Hence "man is made up of truth and belief." And beliefs act automatically or without our volition or conscious knowledge.

> *Now I have no belief but if any person has a belief which they take for truth, I destroy it.*

That is the heart of the Quimby practice. The trouble is indeed in the mind but not in fantasy and imagination but in the form of wrong ideas. His practice was to destroy these ideas and to settle the mind in true ideas. For

> *Whatever idea tends to make us unhappy cannot be true though it may be believed.*

The mind in its ignorance or unknowing has embraced many false ideas or has allowed many false ideas to settle in. These cause distress and misery and must be removed. "Take away the dross from the silver and there shall come forth a vessel for the finer. Take away the wicked from before the throne of the king, and his throne shall be established in righteousness." —Proverbs of Solomon

Quimby removed the false ideas from a patient in two ways: first, by silent concentration learned in his mesmeric days and second, by argument and teaching and reasoning. As far back as the days when he was traveling with Lucius, he was developing the first method:

> *I first get the attention of my subject and endeavoring to exclude all other external influences and drawing their mind to myself, I then work up the sensation I wish to produce upon my subject in my own mind and it is immediately communicated to that of the subject and a correspondent feeling will be the result. It is the simple process of mind acting upon mind. . . .the operator must produce in himself the same sensation which he would communicate to the subject . . . .making health the fixed object of my mind, I never parley or compromise.*

A professional healer once refused the offer of a friend to "pray for you." She said, "No thanks, I don't want any amateurs praying for me." With good reason. For the amateur is only reinforcing the condition by his non-professional handling of the problem. He is likely to be still in the position of ascribing independence to disease and therefore cannot rise to a level in himself that is the exact opposite of the condition he wants to replace. As in so many other fields of endeavor, but especially in this science, a person first has to discipline himself before he can influence another. Any one who studies these fragments of insight left by Dr. Quimby will learn what it is to be professional. People will often request from one whom they consider a professional, "Say a prayer for me," as though prayer was as easy as requesting a pound of fruit at the corner grocery. Consider then how Quimby saw his spiritual work:

> *I have labored harder to control the mind of a person in a diseased state than I ever did in performing any manual labor in my whole life. I have spent hours of hard labor in persuading the mind of a person to return to its body. . . .To cure the sick scientifically is laborious but to cure by book or opinions is nothing. It is merely the science of him who had but one talent which he hid and got others to think and act for him.*

One of Quimby's cases will illustrate how he corrected the mind: The lady was aged. She was so lame. . . .that she could hardly rise from her chair and could take only a step with the aid of crutches. In this condition she had lived some years and her only happiness was in reading and thinking on the Bible. She was a Calvanist Baptist and by her belief she had imprisoned her senses (consciousness) in a creed so small and contracted that she could not stand upright or move ahead.

> *Here in this tomb of Calvin, her senses were laid, wrapt in her creed. Yet in this tomb was Christ or Science, trying to burst the bars and break through the bands and rise from the dead. . . .when she would ask for an explanation of some passage* [in the Bible], *the answer would be a stone, and then she would hunger for the bread of life.*

She thought her condition was due to a fall and so told Dr. Quimby when at last she came to see him. He "sat" with her, explained how she felt and then told her that her trouble was caused by a series of excitements from studying upon what she could not reconcile. She thought much on religious subjects but because she had been taught only the literal meanings, her mind became "cloudy and stagnated." This showed itself in her body by her heavy and sluggish feeling which would terminate in paralysis. She said she could not understand how her belief could make her so numb.

> *I said to her, You will admit I have described your feeling. Certainly, she replied. Then said I, What do you suppose Jesus meant by these words, A little while I am with you, then I go my way and you shall seek for me and where I go you cannot come.*

> *Do you believe that Jesus went to heaven? Yes, she replied. Now let me tell you what I think he meant by those words. I had told her before that in order to cure her I must make a change in the fluids and produce a healthy circulation . . . .you have admitted that I have told you your feelings. Then I was with you in sympathy as Christ was with his disciples. And when I go my way I go into health and am not in sympathy*

*with your feelings. Therefore where I
go you cannot come, for you are in
Calvin's belief, and I am in health.*

This explanation produced an instantaneous sensation and a change came over her mind. The mortal put on immortality or health and she exclaimed in joy, "This is a true answer to my thoughts." Quimby continued explaining scripture and a complete change took place—*"She could rise from her chair as quickly as any person of her age. . . .she walked without her crutches."*

The reader will have noticed Quimby's frequent references to *"*the fluids of the system." This is one of his main ideas which needs our attention before we close this commentary and guide. He had told the lady in the case related above that in order to cure her he "must change the fluids." Apparently his idea of the relation between spirit and body was based on that ancient system that thought of the human body as containing four principal fluids: blood, phlegm, choler or yellow bile, and melancholy, or black bile. A person's disposition or temperament was determined by the relative amount of these fluids in the body. As usual, mundane philosophy bases itself in physiology whereas the spiritual philosophy reasons from thought to thing. In the beginning is the word and the word was God or Maker. But this ancient concept has a certain validity today and we still speak of the four temperaments. The four triplicities in astrology and the deck of cards are surviving evidence of the ancient concept. Modern psychologists find other names for these four. Thus do the archetypal meanings thrust themselves through different idioms in different ages. So yet today phlegm means apathy, indifference, undemonstrativeness. Choler is anger and a hasty temper. Blood is zesty, hearty and full of energy, while melancholy could be called in today's language a sad sack. So Quimby wrote to Mrs. Farrel that as her system changed under his treatment, *"it must produce a chemical change in your breast for the fluids must change."* That is, as your mind or thought or outlook or attitude changes, the chemistry of the body changes responsively and correspondingly.

As we saw in Chapter I, optimistic thought triggers off the production of "up" chemicals or hormones in the blood which then circulate through the whole system, bringing the message of health and vitality to each cell.

So we end as we began: It is all in your mind. But there is a way in which this is true. Without the knowledge of this way, the mind is as ignorant and as bound as before. This book has been about that how and also the why. The why is as important as the how for it relieves the mind of unanswered questions. Quimby answers the questions. He has provided a comprehensive and satisfying philosophy of life. For example, he has answered the old question of good and evil as no other I know has done. When someone asks, Why is there so much cruelty and suffering in this world and why is "truth forever on the scaffold and wrong forever on the throne," let him consider:

> *Man cannot be perfectly well or happy, while he is arriving at the truth, anymore than gold can be pure while in the ore. Chemical changes must take place to purify both. Gold and truth are mixed with dross and error, through which both have to work their way* [gold is an ancient symbol of the divine and perfect self].

He has answered the question of free will with a clarity that delights as it illumines.

> *For we are mere machines in the world to be moved and regulated by the wisdom of God or Science, or by the opinions of mankind.*

Thus man acts as he is acted upon and that which acts upon him is either Wisdom or opinion or some mixture of both. If man's mind is devoted to Wisdom and Wisdom is active there, then man acts in wisdom and he is healthy and happy. As the old teaching says, the mind is to be the garden of God "with every tree that is pleasant to the sight and good for food."

> *This world is a state of mind where man creates whatever he understands from what he hears and sees.*

In the beginning of his experiments with the mind, Quimby sought to find out if there was any wisdom outside of man. He found it. This was God for it made and governed all things. He had already done justly and loved mercy. Now he fulfilled the third requirement and walked humbly with his God (See Hosea 6:8). No longer would he ever attribute intelligence to the human brain or attribute the greatness and wonder of man's works to his enlarged brain. He was a kind of modern Greek who was free in wisdom and because he was free, his accomplishments were great. His mind was like that of Themistocles at Salamis after the battle. Watching the Persian fleet depart, he observed, "It is not we who have done this."

To Quimby the human mind was a medium of ideas. Not the mind but the ideas which ruled it were important. He was a modern Solomon and in his own way would say: *"Wisdom is the principal thing; therefore get wisdom. Exalt her and she shall promote thee."* Moreover, Quimby would agree with Solomon that Wisdom is feminine. The spiritual rib is man's best faculty and the average woman is more spiritual than the average man. The Quimby system embraces three main parts:

1. MIND, which is spiritual matter or matter in flux or constantly changing in response to two kinds of influences. There is no "mind over matter" in Quimby's thinking. Mind and matter are one but in two states: one, spiritual or unformed and the other material or formed.

2. BELIEFS, OPINIONS, of or from the world or race mind which influence the mind with limitation and disease. Ignorance, falsehood, lies.

3. WISDOM, On this page it is at the bottom but in Quimby's system it is the top.

> *Wisdom has never been taken into consideration in regard to man's composition.   But man has been looked upon as a machine, set in motion without any wisdom to guide it; as a locomotive let loose, to run its race and die when its fires go out. All calculations made in regard to keeping man running are made without considering Wisdom at all, but he becomes a machine whose owner is error and he is subject to all the errors which error can invent.*

Now it is time for the reader to go on his own pilgrimage through the writings of Park Quimby, the Clockmaker. Let him tell you how to make a clock and how to keep your own clock running.

9

Quotable Quimby Quotes

Gleaned While Editing:

To suppose we act of ourselves is as absurd as to suppose that a clock keeps time by the weight.

For we are mere machines regulated by wisdom or opinion.

The world of opinions is the old world, the world of science is the new world.

The idea that the Bible teaches another world is false.

I never make war with medicine but [with] opinions.

A disease and an opinion are one and the same.

No phenomenon in the natural world ever produced itself and no irregularity, disturbance or disease in the human body ever was self-created.

Happiness is a reward for something.

A spiritual truth is always shadowed forth by some earthly or literal figure. Thus the Bible is spiritual truth illustrated by a literal thing, but the world accepts the shadow and knows nothing of the spiritual meaning.

This world is a state of mind where man creates whatever he understands from what he hears and sees.

There is no intelligence in the body or in the mind but only in the higher power that governs them.

Nor am I afraid if I listen and take a person's feelings of scrofula and any other disease that I shall have it, for the life of the disease is in the person who believes it.

Matter, in itself is capable of no action, except by chemical process, unless connected with a mind or spirituality.

There is no intelligence in anything that can be seen by the eye; one can only see the working of intelligence in matter.

Cease from arguing about what you do not

understand until you learn what you are talking about.

Neither ignorance nor wisdom acts.

Man has analyzed everything but himself which to him is a complete wilderness.

Mind or matter is like mortar or potter's clay.

Priest and physician—these men stand to society as a mesmerizer to his subject.

Every truth which comes to the senses existed before, while every lie or opinion dates its existence only back to its author.

All ideas contain a substance as much as the food we eat, and these very ideas are what make us sick. They enter the system and help to make up the body which itself is an idea.

So ideas are food for the mind and every idea has its effect on mankind. . . .when I correct the ideas, I cure the sick.

What is real cannot be imaginary. The moment reality begins, imagination ceases.

Knowing how little of a sea or swell it takes to upset our bark, I have to sit and paddle along in breathless silence lest some little billow upset all my labors.

Jesus tried to establish the kingdom of truth in man so that men could teach it, but man was not developed enough to receive it.

There is no such thing as goodness of itself.

We are all part and parcel of each other, that is, in our wisdom or that eternal life which cannot be severed, but our beliefs may hold it in bondage.

. . . .I therefore return your money, leaving it till I have tried my best and accomplished my object; then if you please to send it to me, I will receive it as a gift, not as a fee.

I think I hear you say that a child can be troubled with scrofula and they have no mind; then they have no body or fluids for the fluids are the mind as I said before.

God or Wisdom has never made anything to torment mankind.

To believe a thing is to make it.

To know that you exist is nothing, but to know what disturbs you is of great value to everyone.

I never heard that God was either healthy or sick. God is Wisdom and Wisdom is what man wants to keep him happy and the lack of it is either ignorance or error. If the former then he may be ignorantly happy but error is misery.

Now I have no heaven or hell to go to. When I lie down upon my bed, I do not trouble myself what will happen to me when I am nothing. If I am not anything and do not know it, then I am nothing; but if I am anything, I know it as long as I know anything.

. . . .to teach it is to adapt a language that will convey it to another; this is what I am trying to do.

All the life I admit is my wisdom.

I cannot find any law that God ever made.

Do not teach the child that this is good and

that is bad of itself.

Coughing is a physical effort to get rid of a spiritual cause that cannot be removed in this manner.

I feel the feelings of the sick and I have to arrange language to convey this fact. . . .I also feel the effect which the words of the doctor have had on the patient. I have to make him understand this and then destroy it all by language.

When a person talks about what is in the dark (the other world, disease, cause etc.), he is either deceived himself or is trying to deceive others.

I have seen a thing driving a horse who looked more out of place than he would if he were in the thills and the horse had the reins.

Man believes in heaven and hell as independent of himself [or distant localities], *so he lives in hell all his life trying to get to heaven.*

For twenty years I have never said one word to a patient which, if he believed, would make him worse or cause him one moment's pain or misery.

. . .if a doctor tells a patient that he has a disease (which if he believes makes him worse off), punish the doctor and they would soon learn to keep their tongue from speaking lies and learn to tell the truth or say nothing. I have tried it and know that the principle is right — never to say to a person anything that will, if believed, make him the least disappointed or grieved. If you cannot leave a happy impression, do not leave a bad one. This cannot be done under the old system as it kills the practice. Therefore a reform is necessary

I do not know how to describe true courage for wisdom needs no such word.

When I make war with priests and doctors, I do not attack their character but their platform. Neither do I make the people disbelieve in medicine and acknowledge disease. I strike at the disease first — that is the institution. . . .so with religion. . . .

To believe is to act.

I derive more happiness in developing a person's mind than in all the scientific pursuits I ever followed.

God never made any intelligent pain or ache.

I do not intend to attack any person in particular, but the erroneous ideas of mankind in general.

Disease is the misery of our belief. Happiness is the health of our wisdom.

If money would do it, he would give all. . . .but that won't help the sick man. Then Jesus with no money applies his Christ or religion to the sick and they recover.

The word science is the name of that wisdom which sees through the opinions of man.

Every thought contains a substance either good or bad.

We create the enemy which disturbs us.

I repeat that all there is of us that can be seen is the effect of our belief and our beliefs can be changed.

Science is wisdom in practice.

I talk aloud to the natural man but he is entirely ignorant of my conversation with the one who governs him, who is in him, as the light is in the darkness.

Look at the uncultivated savage and you will not see him creeping around as though he had done some mean, dirty act, like the civilized man. Of all mean looking things a human being that is completely under the medical faculty is the lowest; he is as much a slave as the Negro at the south, and in fact, more so.

The things that God has made are all harmless unless they are interfered with, and then they defend themselves according to the law of their lives; for matter is all for man's good, but if we wish to confine it or direct it, we must do it intelligently or bad results will follow.

The cure depends on your faith. Your faith is what you receive from me.

Mind is matter but mind is not wisdom.

I believe that there is a virtue in medicine, which, when taken by the patient, conveys impressions to the mind and these impressions *often result in the entire restoration of health.*

People cannot understand when they see a thing fall that it does not contain weight.

The senses are just what a person knows. . . .for man's senses are his wisdom. The beast has five senses and a great many human beings not half so many.

If we become acquainted with each other spiritually, there is no need of senses.

By the action of my mind upon my patient in his waking state, I can produce the same results which flow from the taking of medicine. I can produce an emetic or cathartic, a dizziness or pain in the head, relieve pain in any part of the system and restore patients by acting directly upon their minds.

I have been twenty years trying to learn it and teach it and am at times nearly worn out.

Our misery comes from our belief, not the thing believe.

I   have   gone   so   far   that   I   have   reduced

certain states of mind to their causes, as certain as ever a chemist saw the effect of a chemical change.

The true design of all medicine is to lead the mind to certain results and then it, the mind, will restore the body.

Disease is what follows an opinion. It is made up of mind directed by error and truth is the destruction of an opinion.

A truth to a person who cannot understand it is a belief.

Author's Closing Note: The complete writings of P.P. Quimby are in preparation and will appear soon in separate volumes.   *Ervin Seale.*